ABOUT THE AUTHOR

CW01432921

Jenny Se
and leac
finance,

with a degree in Mathematics from the University of Oxford and going on to qualify as an actuary.

Jenny worked in technical actuarial roles and as a pensions and investment consultant before gravitating towards the people side of the business, specialising in leading sales teams for large asset management companies. She now has a portfolio-style career and is a regular speaker, consultant and trainer on resilience, business communication, hybrid working, motivation and workplace culture. She has written four books on motivation at work.

When she is not working or being entertained by her three fabulous sons, Jenny spends her time preparing for a piano diploma, running half-marathons and taking (what she hopes are) beautiful photographs.

@j3nsegal
www.linkedin.com/in/j3nny-segal
www.jennysegal.co.uk

To Peter

That you!

Jeny x

i

"A fabulous book, I lived it and loved it. I could identify with every single theme. Jenny has brought real life examples into the debate, which will continue as we fight to empower the next generation of senior female leaders without disenfranchising men. This journey is not finished yet and I'm excited to see what's next from Jenny"
Laura Chappell – CEO, Brunel Pension Partnership

"This is brilliant. Women should probably all read this book. Men should definitely all read it. I wish someone had given me a copy with my new employee induction pack 30 years ago"
Hugh Cutler – Chief Commercial Officer, Mobius Life

"A must-read, especially for men who want to be better allies. It's insightful, practical, and incredibly engaging. Whether you're a leader, a team member, or just someone who cares about equality and fairness, you'll find the memorable stories, lived experiences, tools and understanding to make meaningful changes"
Calum Cooper – Chair of Partnership Council, Hymans Robertson

"A data-rich examination into what's been achieved and, more importantly, the challenges that still lie ahead"
David Semmens – CIO, Cadro & Non-Executive Director

"Fantastically well-structured and easy to access, with powerful case studies and anecdotes giving credibility and context to the recommendations and reflections. I shall be taking on board many of the insights"
Jeanette Wheeler – Partner & Head of Employment, Birketts

"An important collection of individual testimony from women - the largest I have seen - with much to be learned from both the similarities and differences in their experiences. This book has created a much-needed space to bear witness to some surprisingly recent, but definitely outmoded and unhelpful, working practices"
Annabel Gillard – Organisational Culture & Ethics Expert

"Broad research covering a huge variety of perspectives, giving confidence and practical tips to work through this minefield"
Sally Bridgeland – Financial Services Chair

"Incredibly important. A brave, insightful and honest telling of what women have endured in the workplace, with practical advice on how to make a difference. It should be required reading at onboarding"
Imran Qureshi – Head of North America, WTW

"A highly impressive and important book, collecting and powerfully relaying individual women's personal stories of their challenges and barriers in pursuing their careers. For any man aspiring to be an ally, this book provides a real richness of insights and recommends actions we can and must take to support women"
Robert Baker – Founder and CEO Potentia Talent Consulting and Trustee UN Women UK

"There is no more pressing issue in these times than the eradication of gender bias and prejudice in the workplace. In this rigorous, wryly-observed, and deeply insightful book, Jenny Segal shines a searingly bright light onto modern corporate culture, explaining how it affects women at every turn and why it needs to change. Everyone should read this!"
Dawid Konotey-Ahulu CBE – Redington & Mallowstreet Co-Founder

"It's heartening to see how far we've come, and inspiring to know that today's level of understanding by both genders is such that we can continue to challenge biases and antiquated practices across all industries. Jenny's new book is a must read for all generations, and I hope to be around to see the better world the workplace is destined to become"
Lisa O'Connor – Head of Consultant Relations UK, Lazard Asset Management

On Motivation:

Women & Workplace Culture

Jenny Segal

Produced by Softwood Books

ISBN 978-1-0687666-0-2

For the brilliant, cheerleading women in my working life:

Abbi Leech, Annabel Gillard, Kate Taylor, Larraine Solomon, Lisa Whitfield, Michelle Elstein & Sally Bridgeland

And, of course, my BFF, the extraordinary
Samantha Oakley

Mother Earth I

In memory of my beloved, kind, gentle father

Frank Segal

22ⁿᵈ July 1933 - 25ᵗʰ March 2024

*You live on in your photographs, in our hearts
and in your five exceptional grandchildren.*

Intelligent Wisdom

PREFACE

Being a woman at work is rarely neutral. As this book will show, it can result in both advantages and disadvantages, although mainly the latter, despite the zeitgeist's striving to close the gender pay chasm and achieve meaningful female representation in the senior echelons of companies and their boards.

The aim of this book is to use the wisdom and experience of its contributors to evolve the workplace and drive better outcomes for both women **and** men. There are many benefits for us all, as individuals and as a society, of a world where we are judged on merit rather than gender; this is not a zero-sum game.

Many, many men are already great advocates for women, some of the greatest male allies having daughters of their own and accelerating change for the sake of the next generation. Others have unhelpful unconscious bias, not affording the credibility and respect due to their female colleagues, and this is reflected with terms like 'The Authority Gap' and 'mansplaining' slipping into common parlance. And a small minority continue to cross the line into sexual harassment and we are still finding out the extent of the problem in the wake of the #MeToo movement.

Similar in format to its predecessor volumes On Motivation: Building Better Workplace Cultures, On Motivation: Purpose & Hybrid Working and On Motivation: Board Effectiveness & Culture, this synthesis of the views and opinions of a host of contributors is presented in an informative, crisp and entertaining style. Spiced with quotes, case studies, photographs and cultural references, I have adopted a colour-coded system for ease of reference:

> *"Quotes from my reference group are in blue"*

Case Studies

are in green

LEARNING POINTS

are in lilac

- and are credited here

CHAPTER SUMMARIES

1. are in

2. purple

I hope you find it an enjoyable, entertaining and easy read. But it has a serious purpose: it is a call to arms for women to support each other, for men to support women, and to raise awareness of the unconscious biases from which we all suffer and that are particularly detrimental to working women.

CONTENTS

TABLE OF PHOTOGRAPHS

TABLE OF FIGURES

Women &

Workplace

Culture

What Lies Beneath

1. THE RESEARCH

> *"A lot of business decisions are driven by men. And on balance that means women will lose out because a lot of men only want to deal with men. Whilst some will speak to both men and women, very few will only deal with women"*

1.1 SCENE SETTING

This fascinating chart (Figure 1.1) brilliantly captures the working rhythms of creative geniuses. The descent of the muse is unpredictable, her moments of inspiration to be seized when they arise. Morning, noon, or night, these great minds were able to flex their working patterns around her callings.

At first glance, the chart shows us how varied their routines were, some turning night into day, creating feverishly whilst others slept. Others were early risers, starting their work before the sun was up. Look again and you will notice how little time they spent on the mundanities of life: a day job and tedious, soul-sapping admin. Look closer still and you will see how few of these creative greats were women. Presumably the women of the time were too busy handling all the life admin/domestic chores/child rearing to be creative, let alone have the time and space to get famous for it.

But the balance has changed and continues to change. The workplace's new-found focus on diversity, equity & inclusion (DE&I) is now enabling brilliant women to achieve their potential, smash the glass ceiling and enjoy working on their own terms.

Or is it?

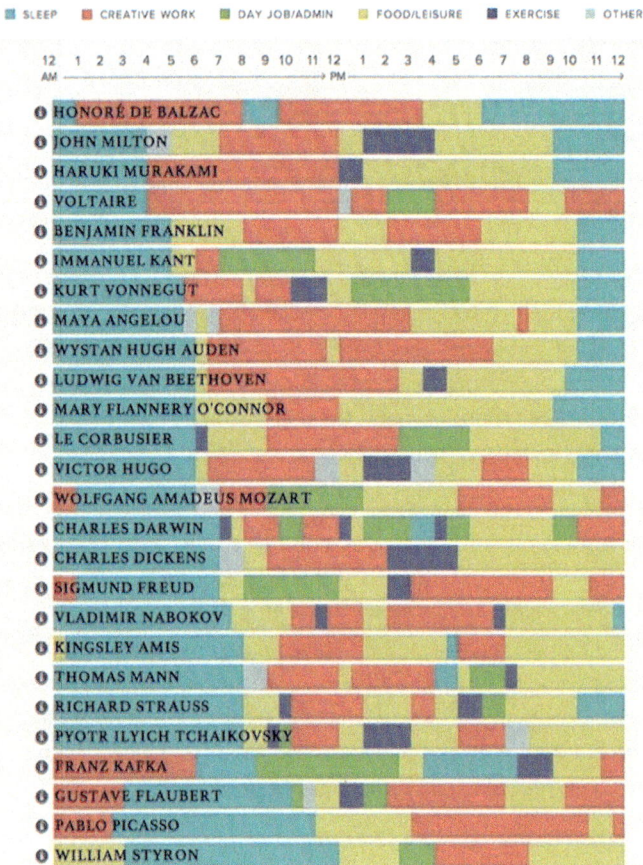

SLEEP   CREATIVE WORK   DAY JOB/ADMIN   FOOD/LEISURE   EXERCISE   OTHER

12 1 2 3 4 5 6 7 8 9 10 11 12 1 2 3 4 5 6 7 8 9 10 11 12
AM   PM

HONORÉ DE BALZAC
JOHN MILTON
HARUKI MURAKAMI
VOLTAIRE
BENJAMIN FRANKLIN
IMMANUEL KANT
KURT VONNEGUT
MAYA ANGELOU
WYSTAN HUGH AUDEN
LUDWIG VAN BEETHOVEN
MARY FLANNERY O'CONNOR
LE CORBUSIER
VICTOR HUGO
WOLFGANG AMADEUS MOZART
CHARLES DARWIN
CHARLES DICKENS
SIGMUND FREUD
VLADIMIR NABOKOV
KINGSLEY AMIS
THOMAS MANN
RICHARD STRAUSS
PYOTR ILYICH TCHAIKOVSKY
FRANZ KAFKA
GUSTAVE FLAUBERT
PABLO PICASSO
WILLIAM STYRON

Podio

Figure 1.1 – The Daily Routines of Famous Creative People
Reproduced by kind permission of Podio®

Women and workplace culture is such a vast subject, filling multiple column inches in multiple guises: from menopause to glass ceilings and glass cliffs, from gender pay gaps to hybrid working, parental leave to domestic abuse, allyship, DE&I, quotas, imposter syndrome, Queen Bee syndrome, positive bias, negative bias, proximity bias. And it's a minefield. Can we share our authentic views without risk of backlash? In fact, given the sensitivities around gender, is it unintentionally divisive even to frame the title as "Women & Workplace Culture"?

There's a lot to discuss. To delve deeper into these areas, during the spring and summer of 2024 I interviewed a group of volunteers[1] to find out their thoughts on women and workplace culture. My goal? To use the research[2] to reimagine workplace cultures that work for women. And also for men.

WHOSE SIDE ARE YOU ON?

The world is better when we are united. And yet we are a world of factions. Do you support Tottenham or Arsenal? Are you a Northerner or a Southerner? Republican or Democrat? Believer or non-believer? We are becoming ever more polarised by the many terrible, contentious issues that our planet is facing. Feeling that we have to pick a side, even when there is overwhelming human suffering on both, when there are no baddies or goodies, just people trying to create safe, happy lives for themselves and their loved ones.

Where does this hardwired tribalism stem from? Perhaps it is our biological roots, evolving on the savannah where belonging to a tribe maximised our chances of survival, a tribe which fed us, looked out for us, protected us from attack.

---

1   None of the volunteers identified themselves as transgender

2   The research and themes presented are limited to those areas actively raised by the volunteers and are confined to their experiences

We are a long way from the savannah now. Yet tribalism pervades our psyche, even when it is unhelpful for our mental health, for our society, for world peace and our very survival as a species. We have forgotten that people are people, and that - surely? - our greatest moral purpose *as* people is to be *pro* people; that we should focus our efforts on minimising human suffering.

During my many months of immersion in this Women & Workplace Culture project, I have become acutely aware of the tightrope I am treading. By flagging issues that affect women, there is a risk of being perceived as anti-men. And by flagging the childbearing issues that affect women, there is a risk of being perceived as anti- trans / post-menopausal / voluntarily childless / involuntarily childless / etc women.

This book is **pro people**. And **anti injustice**.

It needs all of us, ALL of us, to recognise the issues that create problems for women at work. To own them. To tell it how it is.

And it needs ALL of us to be part of the solution. In particular, it needs **men's allyship** to help create a fair environment for women at work and beyond.

MISOGYNY AND WOMANHOOD

To understand the problems women face in the workplace, it is helpful to go back to their source. Misogyny. It has been around since the dawn of time and is reflected in art, literature, human societal structure, historical events, mythology, philosophy and religion worldwide.

misogyny *noun*:

"hatred of, contempt for, or prejudice against women or girls. A form of sexism that can keep women at a lower social status than men, thus maintaining the social roles of patriarchy"

– Wikipedia

A bemused onlooker might well look at today's debate around the definition of 'woman' and think it a stroke of misogynistic genius; after all, how can a group that doesn't clearly exist argue for its rights? It presents an unhelpful distraction from the very real need to address ingrained gender inequalities that affect ALL women.

The rite of passage in attaining womanhood is also very real. It is part of what makes us so empathetic and resilient, what shapes our cognitive diversity. And many women will be familiar with sections of this well-trodden path...

*From the gender bias of our early rearing, when we are dressed in pink, overly cosseted and encouraged to play with Barbies, to the tight one-on-one friendships, and bullying by ostracisation, we experience at school. To the embarrassments of puberty: the blood-stained cushion on your boyfriend's sofa, being wolf-whistled at as you pass a building site, **not** being wolf-whistled at as you pass a building site. To being slut-shamed for sleeping with your boyfriend, or being labelled frigid if you don't. To being less physically strong than your partner; that thud of fear in your chest when you sense someone behind you as you walk home after dark, clutching your keys in case you need them for defence. To being spoken over by those who know less, but whose size and bass tones command an audience. To being terrified that you are pregnant, then later being terrified that you won't be able to get pregnant. The rollercoaster of IVF. The dilemma and anguish around abortion. Hiding your pregnancy for the first three months in case you miscarry, then miscarrying in secret in the toilet at work, without solace, hiding your tears from your colleagues. The irreversible physiological and mental changes brought on by pregnancy and motherhood. The intrusive questions about why you don't have children and, if you do, whether you shouldn't be at home looking after them. To the constant caring - for your home, for your children, for your ageing parents. Then to the hot flushes of menopause, adjusting to no longer being fertile, desirable; becoming invisible.*

We are standing on the shoulders of those giants who came before us and fought hard for our rights - for votes, for contraception, for abortions. For maternity leave, for equal opportunities, for equal pay. They took us a long way, but there is much further still to go.

And that is why I am striving to advance the progress of women in the workplace, by sharing the stories, wisdom and learnings of our 'minority' group, albeit one that accounts for slightly more than 50% of the population.

Girl Power

1.2 PARTICIPANTS

In early 2024, I posted a request for research participants on LinkedIn:

> Do you have 30 minutes to spare to help me with a research project? I'm looking for your thoughts, experiences and perspectives to bring to life my fourth book on motivation: 'Women & Workplace Culture'
>
> There is so much around on this at the moment. In multiple guises. From #menopause to #glassceilings and #glasscliffs, from #genderpaygap to #hybridworking, #parentalleave to #domesticabuse. #allyship, #diversityequityinclusion, #quotas. #impostersyndrome, Queen Bee syndrome, positive bias, negative bias, #proximitybias. And it's a minefield. Can we share our authentic views without risk of being cancelled? In fact, given the sensitivities around gender, am I even allowed to frame the title as "Women* & Workplace Culture"?
>
> There's a lot to discuss. My goal is to use the research to reimagine workplace cultures that work for women. And also for men. And every flavour in between.
>
> So please get in touch if you'd like to take part - the more the merrier. Definitely women of all seniorities. And men who have an interest: male allies, fantastic male bosses who support women. And men who feel excluded by this zeitgeist.
>
> *define in whichever way does not cause you offence

The response was phenomenal.

My post got around 15,000 views and generated 90 research volunteers, of whom 77 - the Women & Workplace Culture 2024 Reference Group (my 'reference group') - booked interviews.

This important topic clearly struck a chord.

DEMOGRAPHICS

Of the participants, the **majority were women**[3] (87%):

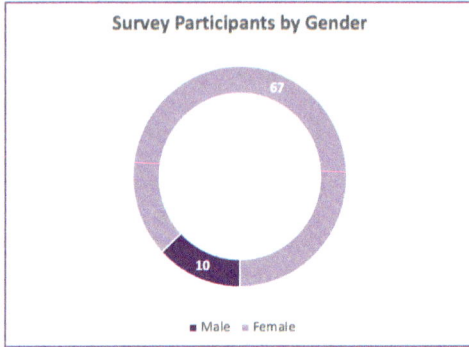

Figure 1.2 - Survey Participants by Gender
Source: Women & Workplace Culture 2024 Reference Group

with a **median age of 47**, the males being on average older (53) than the females (46):

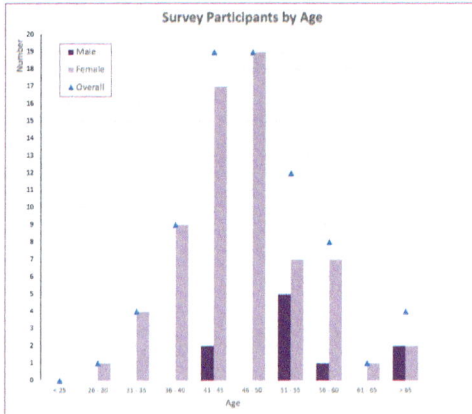

Figure 1.3 - Survey Participants by Age
Source: Board Effectiveness & Culture 2023 Reference Group

---

3   None of the volunteers identified themselves as transgender

Most were from the **financial services sector**:

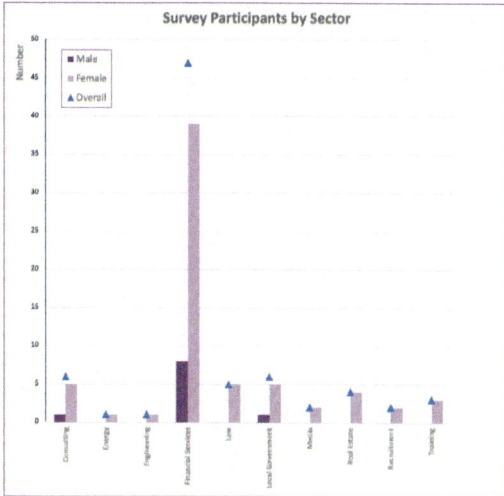

Figure 1.4 -Survey Participants by Sector
Source: Board Effectiveness & Culture 2023 Reference Group

and self-classified as working at a **senior** level.

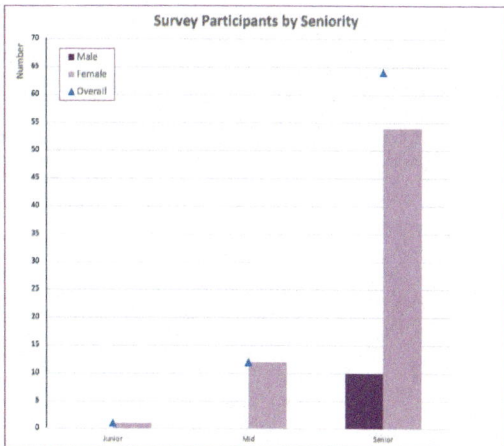

Figure 1.5 - Survey Participants by Seniority
Source: Board Effectiveness & Culture 2023 Reference Group

The stories they generously shared were honest, authentic and sometimes shocking. To protect their identities, and those of the individuals they have referenced, I have not listed them by name. They know who they are, and I thank them whole-heartedly for their contribution to my research.

1.3 THE QUESTIONNAIRE

BRIEFING

Before being interviewed, each participant was briefed:

I will be asking about your experiences as a woman in the workplace or, if you are a man, with women in the workplace.

In advance of our call, please could you consider the following topics (or indeed any others that feel relevant), pick those that resonate and think about what you would like to share.

I am particularly interested in situations that were well-handled and, for those that were not, what would have resulted in a better outcome.

DE&I
- glass ceilings
- glass cliffs
- gender pay gap
- parental leave
- quotas
- imposter syndrome
- image
- "Leaning Out" (not putting yourself forward for a role you are capable of)

Work/Life Balance
- hybrid working
- proximity bias
- domestic responsibilities
- caring responsibilities

Colleagues
- allyship
- Queen Bee syndrome
- mansplaining
- unwanted sexual advances
- unrecognised work (eg team nurturer)

Female Health
- periods
- fertility
- miscarriage
- pregnancy
- menopause
- domestic abuse

QUESTIONS

1. DEMOGRAPHICS

- What is your age?
- What is your gender?
- Would you describe your seniority as Junior, Mid or Senior?
- Which industry/sector do you work in?

2. GENDER BIAS SCALE

On a scale of 1 to 10, where 1 is 'not at all' and 10 is 'hugely', how much has being a woman:

- positively impacted your ability to do your job?
- negatively impacted your ability to do your job?
- positively impacted your career advancement?
- negatively impacted your career advancement?

Why have you arrived at these scores?

3. LIVED EXPERIENCES

Please share a few of your experiences as a woman in the workplace or, if you are a man, *with* women in the workplace.

Where the experience was negative, what would have improved it?

Where the experience was positive, what could others learn?

4. FINAL THOUGHTS

What other thoughts would you like to share?

Pink or Blue?

Copyright © 2024 Jenny Segal

2. GENDER BIAS RESEARCH FINDINGS

2.1 SUMMARY

1. Women perceive that being a woman has a positive impact on their ability to perform their job, with a median score of 8 out of 10 (where 1 is 'not at all', 10 is 'hugely')

2. Their key enablers are possessing a high EQ (empathy in particular), the ability to multi-task, bringing a sense of perspective and being memorable

3. However, they felt that their gender-linked abilities conferred no particular career advantage, with a median score of 5 out of 10

4. They recognise that being a woman can also have a negative impact on their ability to perform their job, with a median score of 6 out of 10

5. The number one blocker is having children, followed by: being under-estimated / spoken over / patronised, feeling there is a boys' club and the discomfort others experience when women exhibit 'masculine' leadership traits

6. Being a woman was seen as having a negative impact on career advancement, with a median score of 6 out of 10

7. Overall women's career advancement does not match their ability, with a median negative gender bias score of -3 (on a scale of -18 to +18)

8. Common experiences as a woman in the workplace coalesced around sexual harassment, the Motherhood Penalty and unequal treatment

2.2 ENABLERS AND BLOCKERS

> *"I would like it if we were gender-blind. If we were viewed as individuals in our own right, rather than being part of two quite separate distributions"*

Just how much does gender bias impact a woman's career? To get an idea of the extent, I asked the women in my reference group to assess how much their gender has impacted both their *ability* to do their job and their *career advancement*, both positively and negatively. And, according to the reference group, being a woman is rarely neutral.

ENABLERS

Overall, the reference group women reported that being a woman has a strongly positive impact on their performance (Figure 2.1).

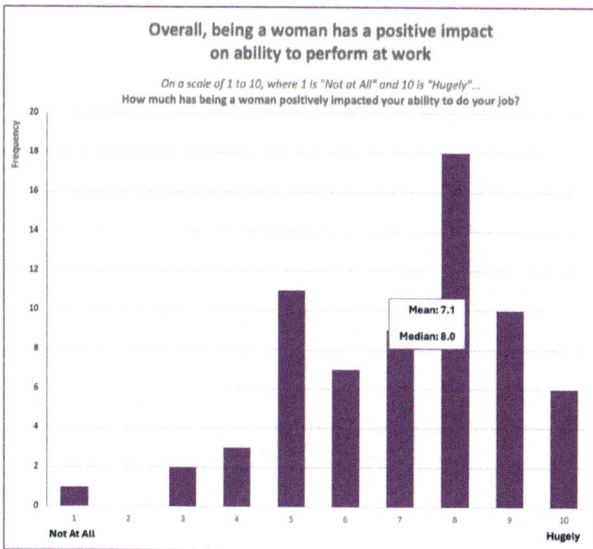

Overall, being a woman has a positive impact on ability to perform at work

On a scale of 1 to 10, where 1 is "Not at All" and 10 is "Hugely"...
How much has being a woman positively impacted your ability to do your job?

Mean: 7.1
Median: 8.0

Figure 2.1 - Positive Impact on Ability to Perform
Source: Women & Workplace Culture 2024 Reference Group Women [67]

Possessing a high EQ, the ability to multi-task, bringing a sense of perspective and being memorable as - frequently - one of very few women in the room, were the most-commonly cited reasons (Figure 2.2).

Figure 2.2 - Abilities and Enablers
Source: Women & Workplace Culture 2024 Reference Group Women [67]

Contrary to popular belief, it is interesting to note research[4] suggesting that males and females actually possess equal levels of overall EQ, although there *are* gendered strengths when EQ is broken down into its component parts. In general, women tend to score higher than men in empathy, emotional self-awareness, interpersonal relationships and social responsibility, whilst men score more highly in assertiveness, stress tolerance and self-regard (confidence).

---

4   Meshkat, M., & Nejati, R. (2017) - Does Emotional Intelligence Depend on Gender? A Study on Undergraduate English Majors of Three Iranian Universities. Sage Open, 7(3)

> *"There's a male ego thing. It's much easier for women to change tack and admit they are wrong"*

> *"Now, being a woman, we can - and are expected to - say things that men can't. Introducing concepts, and the importance of people, into processes. We spend more time than men watching the dynamic when everyone else is speaking. We don't have that many words, so we make our interventions count"*

But the reference group women felt that their gender-linked abilities conferred no particular career advantage (Figure 2.3), despite some benefiting from the drive to get more women into senior roles and onto boards.

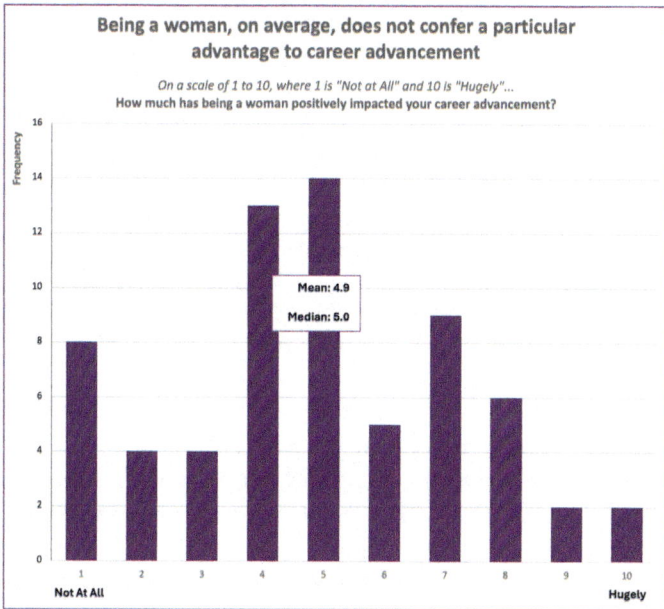

Figure 2.3 - Positive Impact on Career Advancement
Source: Women & Workplace Culture 2024 Reference Group Women [67]

Being a woman can also negatively impact one's ability at work (Figure 2.4).

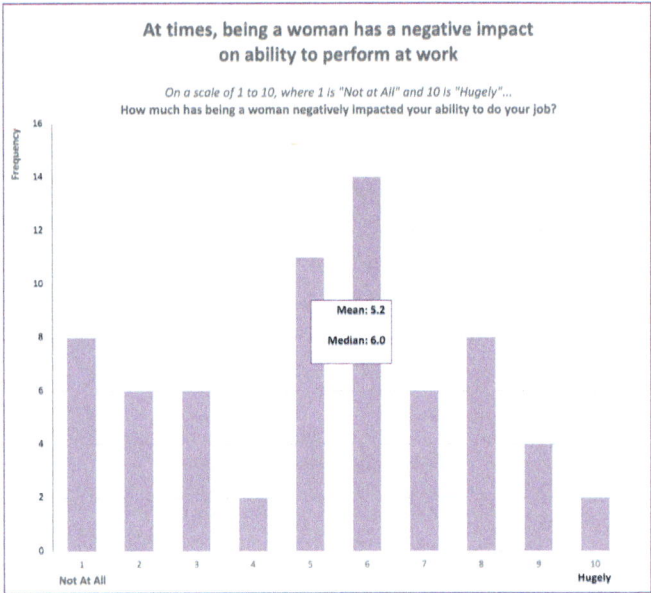

Figure 2.4 - Negative Impact on Ability to Perform
Source: Women & Workplace Culture 2024 Reference Group Women [67]

Perhaps unsurprisingly, the number one perceived blocker is having children (Figure 2.5): the anticipation of an extended period of maternity leave, actually being out of the office on maternity leave and then bearing the brunt of the childcare responsibilities on return. Then came being under-estimated, talked over and patronised, and feeling that there is a boys' club from which women are excluded. Dissonance was also seen as a problem: the discomfort that can be felt (by both genders) when women exhibit traits that are lauded in men, such as being ambitious, driven and assertive, but clash with stereotypical feminine behaviours. And there were reproductive issues, such as endometriosis, IVF, pregnancy and menopause.

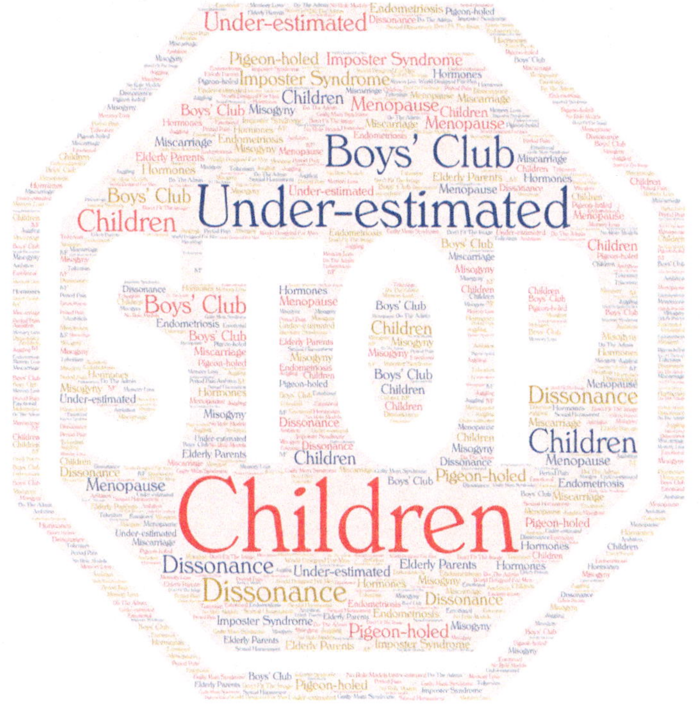

Figure 2.5 - Disablers and Blockers
Source: Women & Workplace Culture 2024 Reference Group Women [67]

As a result, more often than not, being a woman was seen as having a negative impact on career advancement (Figure 2.6).

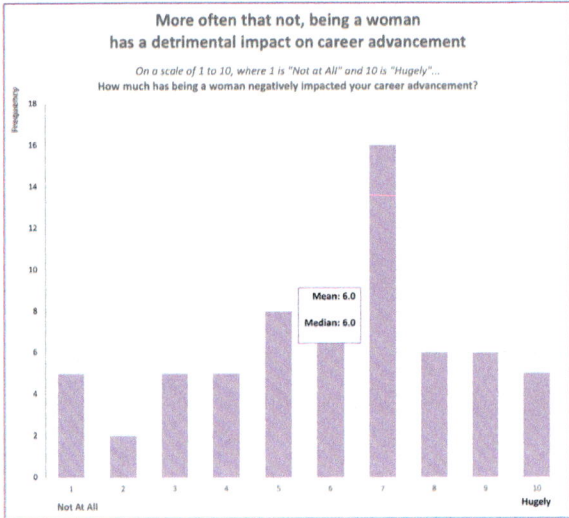

Figure 2.6 - Negative Impact on Career Advancement
Source: Women & Workplace Culture 2024 Reference Group Women [67]

2.3 GENDER BIAS SCALE

I then took these two sets of self-assessed paired scorings and subtracted the career advancement score from the ability score, to give a **Gender Bias Scale**[5]: a measure of how much women *perceive* their gender has hindered their career progression. In other words, it provides a proxy for the gender bias they feel they have experienced.

Figure 2.7 charts the gender bias scores for the reference group women. Zero is neutral, i.e. the subject perceives that her career advancement has been appropriate for her level of ability.

---

5   The Gender Bias Scale ranges from -18 (strong negative bias) to +18 (strong positive bias) and I have calculated it as:
Positive impact on career advancement LESS Positive impact on ability to perform PLUS
Negative impact on ability to perform LESS Negative impact on career advancement

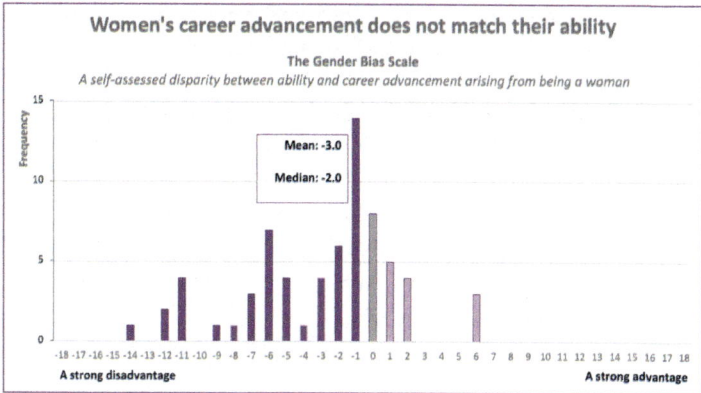

Figure 2.7 - Gender Bias Scale
Source: Women & Workplace Culture 2024 Reference Group Women [67]

A positive score indicates a perceived discrimination in favour of women and there was some, largely arising from the drive to get more women into senior positions. Conversely, a negative score indicates a perceived bias against women and this was felt to be much more prevalent, despite these recent drives to improve the status quo.

Collectively there has been clear experience of perceived gender bias, with a mean score of -3.0 and a median of -2.0. Sadly, the women in my reference group felt that their career advancement did not match their ability.

2.4 KEY THEMES

EMOTIONAL INTELLIGENCE

> *"There have been countless times when having the skills not to react is good. Men are jumping up and down, banging the table.*
> *I am alpha-driven, but with female traits.*
> *It's paid so many dividends"*

> *"As I get older, I realise there are skills I have that I
> wouldn't have if I were a man. It's about building teams,
> doing good, purpose, ethos. I am a more empathic, better
> leader. If I were a man, I would have been more alpha"*

When asked which of their natural female traits impact their ability at work, high emotional intelligence got a regular mention. That combination of innate 'soft' skills - caring, nurturing and empathy - coupled with an efficiency, sense of proportion and ability to multi-task - often arising from juggling domestic and work responsibilities - make women very valuable indeed: they are often loyal, dedicated, obliging workhorses who act as diplomats and don't like to rock the boat.

> *"If you want something done, ask a busy person! Women bring
> a need for balance, a respect for boundaries. We are often
> responsible for a homestead and other people's schedules.
> This is one of the most valuable skills we bring to the table"*

But this is often the rub. And a double rub, at that. Firstly, their 'soft' skills are frequently discounted, not seen as valuable as the 'hard', more masculine-attributed skills of sales, negotiation and tough decision-making. Then their willingness to take on additional work means they can be taken advantage of, getting dumped with lower-value projects that compromise bandwidth for the higher profile work which would allow them to shine and get noticed.

> *"We are not fully recognised for what we bring. We are
> good mothers, good sisters. Businesses need to be nurtured.
> This doesn't fit into the view of 'strong' leadership which
> is biased against women. We should redefine leadership
> so that it is about being human, vulnerable, caring"*

But having high emotional intelligence can carry with it the taint of being highly emotional. And no one likes to see high emotion in the workplace. Our fears of emotional displays tend to be stereotypically gendered; we worry about anger erupting from men and women dissolving into tears.

> *"I have a total fear of making women cry"*

> *"I have seen women being emotional in the workplace and they have castigated themselves about it. It's ok for us all to show emotion. Whenever you allow someone to express emotion about something that's bothering them, you might 'lose' time during that day, but with women you always get it back"*

> *"Our biological make-up, our caring nature, our female attributes can be taken advantage of. We shouldn't be judged on male standards. Being emotional is not bad, it means we are empathetic. We are held to a different standard because men don't know how to deal with it"*

There is a particular suspicion that if a woman gets too upset, it compromises her ability to make rational decisions.

> *"For many women, tears come quite easily. Once when I was younger, I was intensely frustrated by a work situation and I cried. Men don't like women who cry and it changes their perception of them. People remember periods of high emotion and I got rated down on the basis that I was not rational enough. It taught me to be less trusting.*
>
> *As I've got older, I've gained context about what's important and I've realised that emotion is incredibly powerful, provided you are in control of it, rather than it being in control of you. Now I think: 'How do I get the outcome I want by using that emotion?' It's a kind of meta-awareness and requires a lot of self-reflection"*

With complete free reign over the number and variety of issues to raise, it was interesting that the research group's comments coalesced around three key nexuses:

Sexual Harassment: Whilst the trend has improved, 40% of the women in the reference group explicitly mentioned suffering sexual harassment at work. This continues to be the case, despite the heightened awareness of its unacceptability in the wake of #MeToo.

The Motherhood Penalty: The suspicion that they will disappear off to have children affects women in multiple ways. Earlier in their careers, they are not considered for opportunities just in case they get pregnant. They lose ground and confidence when they are on maternity leave. Then when they do return there is the expectation that they will have more children *and* that they are less committed because they are bearing the childcare load, and so they are passed over for promotion. All of these compound the gender pay gap and toughen the glass ceiling, a horn effect[6] that ripples through age cohorts, colouring how women are perceived irrespective of their age or fertility.

Inequality: This covers a gamut of issues, from not being viewed as credibly as male peers of equal experience and expertise, to not being considered for promotion fairly or as quickly as male counterparts, to being paid less.

In the rest of this book, I explore these - and other - themes in more depth, suggesting practical ways that we can all work together to change both the narrative and the reality for women at work.

---

6   a cognitive bias that causes one's perception to be unduly influenced by a
     single negative trait, cf. halo effect

Strawberries & Cream

3. LET'S TALK ABOUT SEX

3.1 SUMMARY

1. We judge people on their appearances. Women's wider range of workplace wardrobe options confers them an advantage - a superpower - that they can use to dial up their authority

2. Sexual harassment is still worryingly prevalent. Sometimes it is flirtation gone wrong or misjudged, but often it is not

3. Because it is so commonplace, we have become desensitised to sexual harassment. Examples of reverse harassment (in which women have harassed men) can reawaken us to its inappropriateness

4. Incidents involving clients or suppliers are particularly difficult to handle, with businesses conflicted by commercial considerations

5. Good colleagues will be on the alert, ready to step in to defuse a situation before it becomes serious. Simple, effective interventions include calling out inappropriate banter, joining a conversation that looks to be becoming intense and standing in the way of the harasser

6. Adopting an 'Ask for Angela'-type code phrase could enable employees to subtly seek help from colleagues

7. Businesses could introduce compulsory training and attestations as part of an annual 'Fit & Proper' checklist to raise awareness of sexual harassment

8. Reporting a situation after it has occurred is fraught with difficulties, including not being believed. Businesses must up their game to make the reporting process as painless and as responsive as possible, with the aims of proportionately sanctioning the harasser to prevent them reoffending, and sending a clear message that such behaviours are unacceptable

9. Prevention is better than cure. Some universities have introduced training programmes to great effect, dramatically reducing the number of sexual harassment claims. Their power is in their inclusivity, using the 'Tea and Consent' video to educate, making it clear that we are all at risk of harassment and that we are all responsible for spotting it and intervening

10. Many businesses focus on 'protect the business from being sued' rather than 'do the right thing for the employee'. Treating employees well during sensitive times may well generate loyalty and goodwill that would negate the risk of legal action

3.2 OUR SUPERPOWER

"When I started on the trading floor as graduate in 1992, there was very much a glass ceiling - no senior women, no role models. There were vastly more men than women and you had to dress in a certain way, be slim, attractive, well turned out. What you looked like had an impact"

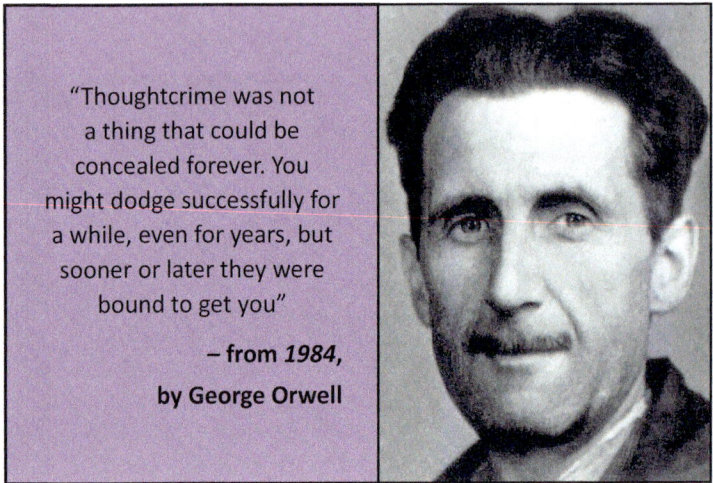

"Thoughtcrime was not a thing that could be concealed forever. You might dodge successfully for a while, even for years, but sooner or later they were bound to get you"

– from *1984*,
by George Orwell

Figure 3.1 - George Orwell
Source: pixabay

George Orwell's dystopian classic made viscerally plain the horrors of repression and mind control. Fortunately for us, 'thoughtcrime' is entirely legal in modern society. We are free to think what we like, to let our minds wander, to enjoy the creativity and escapism that imagination and inspiration bring. There is no need to curb the random, often reflexive, thoughts that pop in and out of our consciousness, even if they are unwanted, disturbing or distressing. And as long as these thoughts do not spill over into actions, all is good.

The reason this is relevant to the discussion is contentious. But there are no sacred cows here and just because something is contentious does not make it less true: **men are biologically programmed to be visually stimulated in a way that women aren't**[7]. The sight of a

---

7   Chung, W., Lim, S., Yoo, J., Yoon, H. Gender difference in brain activation to audio-visual sexual stimulation; do women and men experience the same level of arousal in response to the same video clip? International Journal of Impotence Research 25, 138–142 (2013)

woman in revealing clothes is distracting for heterosexual men in a way that is not fully mirrored when genders are reversed. And this can create issues in the workplace.

> *"There was a complaint against a man in the office for inadvertently glancing at his female colleagues' breasts. The matter was discussed at the most senior level and the individual was spoken to. He was mortified and asked to apologise but was unable to, so as to preserve the complainants' anonymity. Conversely no one spoke to - or was allowed to speak to - the women involved to suggest that they stop wearing clingy, low-cut tops to work"*

The bottom line is that women have a superpower when they are dealing with heterosexual men. Some use it unwittingly; some use it cynically. Some are too PC[8] to countenance it. And some wish it didn't exist. But it does. To ignore it is folly and doesn't make it go away.

DRESS TO IMPRESS

> *"I would get comments about me tottering along in my high heels. But it's almost a part of the smart dress code. Sexualising workwear for women"*

There is an interesting dichotomy in traditional office wear. Men wear suits: a shirt, jacket and trousers, maybe a tie. The standard woman's outfit is sexier: figure-hugging trousers and pencil skirts, high heels. This is magnified when we look at the dress code for fancy evening events, the man in his tuxedo and bow tie - simply a more formal version of his day wear - whilst the woman is required to wear an evening dress, generally designed to emphasise feminine beauty, exposing shoulders, cleavage, back and leg. Does it matter?

---

8   politically correct

Case Study: A Workshop on How to Dress Professionally

I attended a workshop for women on how to dress professionally. With minimal words, the trainer asked us to guess her income bracket, education level, car and interests from multiple-choice lists. Based on nothing at all apart from a few spoken words and how she looked, we had all pegged her as better-educated, richer and more successful than she actually was.

Then she showed us how. One-by-one, she took off her accessories: her Hermes scarf, her jacket, belt, earrings, lipstick. And with the removal of each item, she shrank before our eyes, becoming increasingly less impressive and less credible. It taught me an invaluable lesson I have carried with me throughout my career: image matters.

Image matters, irrespective of gender. Subconsciously, we are all making value judgements about each other all the time based on how we present ourselves, and that includes how we speak, how we dress, our make of pen, the quality of our shoes. And manufacturers know it and advertisers play on it, hence the power of brand.

Women have more wardrobe dimensions to play with than men. And because of this there is much greater scope for variability in the first impressions women make. Whilst this might sound like an unfair disadvantage, it doesn't have to be. Because, whilst it is certainly unfair, it doesn't have to be negative: it can swing positively too, if you are aware of it, take control of it, own it. It gives women a superpower that men don't have, an additional dimension to influence how we are perceived, how much power and influence others ascribe to us. Yet many women don't make the most of the impact that they could have, even though they are unwittingly judged by others all the time based on nothing more than what they happened to throw on that morning.

> *"It helps that I'm tall - it gives me more gravitas. I can choose to wear heels and be scary. I have the option to dress in a way that enables me to control the room"*

> *"On the conference circuit, people dismissed me because I used to let my hair down and have fun. So when I started speaking at the conferences, people had already formed their impression of me. One of the audience commented: 'Who is that woman nearly wearing a dress?'"*

Once you get to a position of seniority that you are happy with where your name and your brand command respect, you can dress how you like.

> *"The senior partner looked like the cleaning lady. You would never have guessed how rich and successful she was"*

But whilst you are still aspiring, it is an easy win to assess how your image is coming across and whether it is helping or hindering you. It shouldn't be like this, but things aren't always the way they should be. Thoughtcrime is not illegal.

> *"Your authority is inversely proportional to the length of your skirt"*

49

WHEN FLIRTATION CROSSES THE LINE

> *"Sexual harassment is very personal. It's about having respect for someone's boundaries, for what makes them feel uncomfortable. I once had to handle a complaint from an individual about someone staring inappropriately into her eyes. I spoke to him directly and explained the impact this was having on her"*

Banter and gentle flirtation may be a glorious part of everyday life, the simple joys of interacting with our fellow humans. But in a workplace context, there is potential for them to go horribly wrong.

The misfiring can be innocent, through misreading a situation or clumsy execution. Or it can be more sinister, if there is a power imbalance or an underlying current of misogyny. And most of us can easily discern the difference, with a pretty good handle on when an interaction is acceptable, when it is borderline and when it is wildly inappropriate.

> *"Flirting is fine, but when there is a power imbalance, it is crucial to make sure the person is happy with the engagement, as you're likely to be working together for a long time. It's the same as if the CEO invites you to play golf on a Sunday - it can be very hard to refuse. Don't put someone in a position where they feel they can't say no"*

> *"I introduced myself to my client's colleague, saying I thought we had met before. He replied, 'Are you the mother of one of my children?'"*

> *"A young female graduate was in a bar after work, socialising with her new colleagues, when one of the more senior men in the group grabbed her waist. In a non-work situation, she would have had the choice of accepting his advances or telling him to get lost. But because of the power imbalance, she had no choice - she felt she couldn't object and just had to put up with it"*

It is infuriating and frustrating that people still behave like this, despite workplace policies and heightened awareness. Perhaps there is confusion over when work stops and play starts, as people forget the reality that the 'workplace' extends way beyond the walls of the building your desk sits in: it is anywhere where you are with your colleagues, be that the office, the pub, an awards dinner, a team training session or an outing with an overnight hotel stay.

Situations can get particularly difficult when the problem is with very senior men, particularly the owner or the CEO. If re-educating and/or disciplining is ineffective, exiting them from the business generally requires the involvement of the chair and the board.

Just as it is wrong and unconscionable to suggest that a rape is the fault of a person's dress choice, it is unacceptable to victim-blame in cases of sexual harassment. We absolutely cannot question why people are out drinking with their colleagues at 11pm, particularly when networking and relationship-building are often key to professional success. That said, many women have learnt the hard way and so exclude themselves from these high-risk work/social situations and thus damage their potential to build valuable business connections. Or they make a point of *not* drinking so that they have their wits about them should the need arise, and risk being criticised or ostracised for being no fun.

Case Study: Sexual Assault

I was raised in a genderless way, to always feel like a person rather than being aware of my sex. I was the only woman in the team and it was never an issue until a more senior man joined, ten years older than me. We were at the pub and I was being teased by two male colleagues for my terrible darts playing. He joined in but took it too far, testing to see if he could say something that would really hurt me and calling me a '[nationality] whore'. I was more upset at my nationality being used as an insult than being called a whore - I'm not a whore, but I am [nationality] and it is low to insult someone based on their race.

Another time, we were talking in a group with two male partners present when he said: *"I can't tell this story, she would need to leave the room"*. I challenged him, saying this was sexist and that there are things that are appropriate to say at work and things that aren't; they are not based on gender. But no one said anything to back me up and I ended up leaving the conversation.

After another social event, as we left together at the end of the evening, he grabbed my top and pulled it down, exposing me on the street. When I remonstrated, he asked why I was making such a big deal about it, saying that I was so playful, that I only hang out with men and blaming me for being flirty.

I can look after myself, but he was managing a young, shy girl and I was worried for her. He had crossed a physical line with me, so I felt I had to speak to HR. It was a very gruelling experience. There were two witnesses to the assault, but one of them withdrew because he was worried about the impact it would have on his career. I was made to repeat my side of the story five times to the same man, who insinuated that I had done something wrong, asking whether I had encouraged my aggressor, for example by touching his arm. I said that even if I had, would that justify me being called a [nationality] whore, excluded from conversations and exposed on the street at night? I was then told that if I felt more comfortable, I could work from home whilst they concluded their investigation. I asked if they were joking - it was him who should be excluded from the workplace, not me!

In the end, the man was fired. But the process took a month and a half and was hugely damaging for me too; I left about four months later. I was told I couldn't speak to anyone about it, but I refused, saying that he had brought shame on me. It has changed me. I'm much more guarded now and I don't feel I can be myself at work anymore.

TURNING THE TABLES

Sexual harassment is such a common occurrence that it is easy to become desensitised to its impact. A different perspective can help to remind us.

"I was sitting next to a senior female chair of trustees. As I took my place next to her, she said: 'I didn't know I'd be having a good-looking young man sitting next to me'. It felt very uncomfortable to be objectified. And it felt like she was displaying her power and influence"

Case Study: Challenging the Stereotypes

Gossip is interesting! We want to believe it. And we tend not to question its veracity, even when the central players are reported to be acting out of character. In fact, that can make it all the more salacious and gossip-worthy.

I was at a conference setting up a stand with a junior female colleague, 30 years younger than me, very attractive and very aware of it. She was being flirtatious, and I felt incredibly uncomfortable and did my best to keep my distance. That evening we had dinner together. She had undone her buttons and was eating her food suggestively. She told me she had just split up with her boyfriend because he was too immature and that she liked older men. It was a very difficult situation: I was unsure whether to just sit there and ignore it or to confront it. I decided to move the conversation on, telling stories about my children and wife.

As we were leaving the restaurant, I was relieved to see some colleagues and went over to join them. She was reluctant and wanted us to go back to the hotel instead, so we parted company. My colleagues commented: *"You're punching above your weight!"* That night as I tried to sleep, I was making excuses for her behaviour and was dreading the next day, but she didn't come down to breakfast and didn't engage with me at all.

Back at the office, a colleague asked if I'd had a good time at the conference, that he'd heard the gossip and said: *"You didn't do anything stupid did you? You're not coming out of this very well."*. I was really worried. I could have gone to our Head of HR but I didn't think I would be believed. Instead, I told a female friend, who was senior, more mature and a good judge of character. She was not surprised and told me she'd nip it in the bud. I was very grateful for her allyship.

In her 2016 novel 'The Power'[9], Naomi Alderman imagines a genetic mutation which enables women to generate powerful electrical currents, conferring a biological advantage that reverses the gender power dynamic. In particular, it enables women to force men to have erections. The rape scene depicted is deeply shocking *because* of the gender reversal, really bringing home the horrors of the violation in a way that we may have become desensitised to when the victim is a woman.

9   The Power, Naomi Alderman, Penguin 2016

> *"I was talking to a client at a conference, standing alongside a senior individual from our PR company who was 20 years older than me. Out of nowhere, he said to me: 'I'm going back to my hotel room - are you coming with me?' It was so unprofessional and embarrassing. I complained to our Head of Europe, who simply told me that I wouldn't have to deal with that individual again. No action was taken against him. He certainly wasn't fired"*

> *"A client was groping my knee under the table at a conference dinner - he was in his 70s and I was in my 20s. It's very tricky when it's a client and it's in public, as public shaming doesn't help. So you either have a moment of brilliance and come up with the perfect put-down or you beat yourself up afterwards. I just moved my chair, but I should have flagged it and swapped seats with a male colleague. But that doesn't stop the behaviour. We should write to the offenders afterwards, saying we won't be inviting them again, even though their firm is important"*

It is challenging enough for complaints to be taken seriously and handled well when the offender is an employee. It is that much harder when the unwanted behaviour comes from an important client or business partner, where there are very tangible commercial risks to intervention.

> *"An important prospect talked down to a senior female colleague and went on to pat her bum. We didn't pursue the business opportunity"*

> *"When it comes to money, business is perpetuated when it shouldn't be. We worked with an Australian distribution partner and they consistently ignored me and treated me disrespectfully. In a meeting I was supposed to be leading, they gave me the coffee order. With my manager's blessing, I complained to HR but no action was taken because this organisation was bringing in the money and it wasn't worth rocking the boat for something that couldn't be perfectly evidenced. Had the perpetrator been internal, it would have been treated more seriously"*

Researching the ESG standards and behaviours of your supply chain and issuing them with a written code of conduct may feel draconian, but helps to send an important message as to what is and isn't acceptable.

> *"A senior male at our largest client invited a young account executive up to his hotel room. They were both drunk, he made sexual advances, she was naive, he wouldn't let her leave. She reported it to HR the next day and the police got involved. We fired the client. The contract was for millions, so it was a very scary decision commercially, but it was the right thing to do"*

Case Study: Wrong-footed at a Conference

I was at a conference waiting for the first speech of the day. I was the only woman at my table; I knew six of my neighbours and I recognised the seventh but could not place him. So I introduced myself, saying I was sure that we had met before, to which he replied: *"Perhaps you were in my bedroom last night and I just don't recognise you with your clothes on."* I was stunned and embarrassed by the sudden sexualisation of the conversation and by being demeaned and objectified. I was very aware that I was surrounded by men, all of whom had heard and not one of whom spoke up in my defence. Then, suddenly, *thankfully*, I remembered how I knew him. And it was perfect: *"I know where we've met before"*, I said, *"You're married to my cousin!"* At that moment, the lights dimmed and he frantically started texting his wife. When the talk ended, as if by magic he was a different person, charming and polite, remembering our family connection and enquiring after my health.

When I got back to the office, I told my boss in an 'It's all in a day's work' kind of a way, not expecting for a moment that he would do anything about it. But he took it very seriously. He rang up the CEO of the company the individual worked for and reported his behaviour. Then he rang up the conference organisers, who banned him from attending future events. I was astounded. I felt incredibly validated and supported.

Sadly, too often the recipient of unexpected and unwelcome comments does not have such a ready and fortuitous comeback. Stunned into silence, feeling humiliated, embarrassed and defensive and not wanting to look like a prude, the natural response is to try to laugh it off and move on as quickly as possible. But this is inevitably followed by an agonising post-event analysis, mulling over the interaction, thinking of things that could and should have been said, if only inspiration had struck in the moment.

We - and those who are witnesses - need a playbook of stock responses, to help us to **defuse** the situation live, to **report** the perpetrator after the event so that they are in no doubt about the inappropriateness of their actions, and to build a culture to **prevent** similar behaviours occurring in future.

3.4 INTERVENTIONS

DEFUSE

To defuse a situation, we have to first be aware of it. Sometimes the affected person might ask for help, but great colleagues will be on the look-out so that they can proactively step in. Simple techniques such as calling out jokes or banter that is inappropriate, joining a conversation that is taking an unwelcome turn or standing between your colleague and their harasser may be all that is needed to resolve the problem quickly and quietly.

"A group of us were entertaining guests at Wimbledon. Over dinner, a much older male client was putting his hand on a female colleague's knee under the table. She flagged it to me and didn't want to make a fuss - plus it would have been pretty bloody awkward to do so - so I simply suggested that all the hosts rotate seats and the immediate problem went away. But I never said anything to him afterwards, something I still regret: I was too young and lacked the confidence. So whilst I was pleased that I had defused that particular situation, I didn't prevent him from doing the same thing to someone else"

Workplaces might consider adopting an 'Ask for Angela'-type code phrase that would allow employees to flag harassment live, alerting colleagues who could step in to avert a problem as it is developing.

REPORT

Reporting involves flagging the problem after the event to a colleague, your boss, their boss or to Human Resources with a view to sanctioning the individual and/or modifying their behaviour so that they do not reoffend.

> *"I worked at an organisation with very little psychological safety. Seniors had secretaries sitting on their laps, feeding them drinks, but I never called it out: I hadn't been there very long, they were all long-serving males and I wasn't as confident in my abilities. It wasn't a culture I liked and I only lasted two years. There was similar bad behaviour in the place I moved on to: three senior males lining up shots for the girls, one of whom was vomiting; a dinner deteriorating into a discussion about who was sleeping with whom, all senior people, all married. And those times I did call it out. If I hadn't, I'd have been condoning it. And it didn't do my career any harm"*

Case Study: A Graceful Resolution

I gave a sports massage to a client that I trained at the gym. I was in my 20s, he was in his mid 40s. He didn't wear underwear during the massage, got an erection several times and walked around the treatment room with no clothes on. I didn't feel threatened; I just thought he was showing off his body, his power.

However, I was concerned that the same thing would happen with my younger female colleague, so I told the manager of the gym, who offered to speak to him and to take him on as a client, but I didn't think either was necessary. Instead, he documented my complaint and sent out an email that looked as if it had been sent to everyone but was actually just sent to this particular client, setting out the gym's policy that you must wear underwear during a massage. It worked.

PREVENT

Many of us meet romantic partners through work so, pragmatically, intimate workplace relationships can, do and should be allowed to flourish. However, one's work colleague may not be the ideal candidate for a casual fling: at best, you will see them on an ongoing basis in the regret-tinged cold light of day and, at worst, the dalliance is fraught with career risk. So if you are serious about a liaison with a workmate, it is crucial to get it right. This means moving slowly and carefully, all the more so the greater the power and age imbalance, to avoid accusations of sexual harassment and lack of consent.

Sexual harassment is not confined to the workplace, nor to the middle-aged hitting on their youngers. The problem is notably prevalent amongst first year university student peers, as teenagers experience new-found freedoms, living away from home with the potential for sexual encounters. In 2015, a National Union of Students poll showed that almost half of the new students in the UK had either experienced or witnessed sexual harassment in their first week of term.

Case Study: Combatting Sexual Harassment at University

Like many universities, the London School of Economics (LSE) University had a recurring problem with sexual harassment claims, with complaints spiking after Rag Week10 each year. So they took preventative action grounded in education and awareness.

All students are required to complete online training about consent and then to attend a workshop discussion group. Run by third year students, part of its brilliance is that it is blame-free with no divisive *'Men as perpetrators, women as victims'* narrative. Instead, everyone is placed on the same side by showing students how to spot unwelcome behaviours and teaching them how to intervene.

The outcome was astonishing. The year after the training was introduced, there were no Rag Week sexual harassment claims.

Businesses could learn a lot from the LSE's approach to help nudge behaviours, perhaps adopting compulsory training and attestations as part of an annual 'Fit & Proper' checklist for completion by all employees.

---

10   an annual event in many universities where students engage in unusual activities to raise money for charity

> *"At conferences, there are a lot of older males and younger females, with lots of behaviour that wasn't notable or unusual, but would be uncomfortable, like touching shoulders, elbows. People are generally aware and supportive and go out of their way to defuse it, by identifying the offenders and standing in their way"*

> *"There is wide-spread acceptance that sexual harassment occurs. There should not be wide-spread acceptance that it is acceptable. We should have training. Staring and stroking count as sexual harassment. Society needs to be told"*

TFL CAMPAIGN

According to UN research[11], 71% of women of any age said they had experienced sexual harassment in public spaces. That figure rises to 86% among 18-24-year-olds, with similar findings across numerous similar studies. Nearly half of those who experience sexual harassment do not tell anyone.

In 2021, TfL[12] launched a poster campaign on London's public transport network 'to challenge the normalisation and dismissal of sexual harassment as something that "just happens"' (Figure 3.2). It highlighted the following as examples of behaviours that are unacceptable:

1. **Cat calling:** making unsolicited remarks of a sexual nature about someone

2. **Exposing:** revealing intimate body parts

3. **Cyber-flashing:** sending or showing sexual content without consent

---

11 'Prevalence and reporting of sexual harassment in UK public spaces', APPG for UN Women, March 2021

12 Transport for London

4. **Pressing:** rubbing against someone on purpose

5. **Touching:** touching someone inappropriately

6. **Staring:** intrusive staring of a sexual nature

7. **Upskirting:** taking photos under someone's clothing.

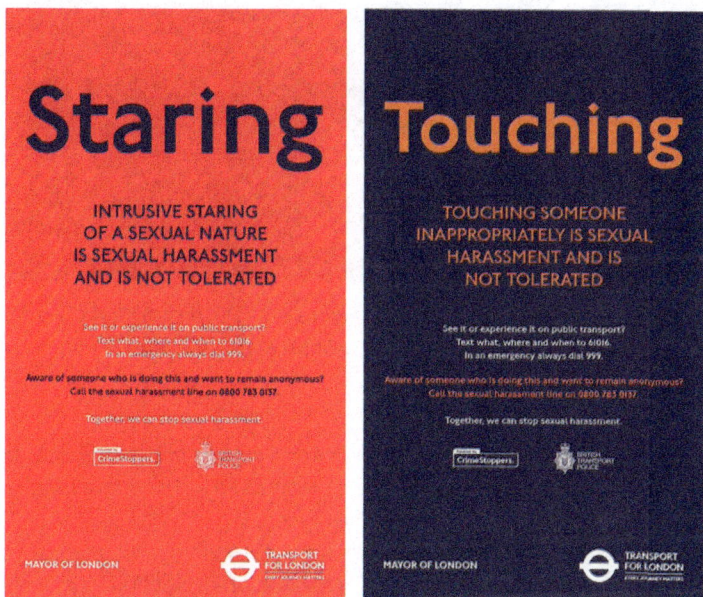

Figure 3.2 - Inappropriate Staring and Touching are Sexual Harassment
Source: TfL 2021 Poster Campaign

Similar to the effective approach adopted by LSE, TfL subsequently went on to encourage the public to be active bystanders, looking out for fellow passengers and intervening when it is safe to do so (Figure 3.3).

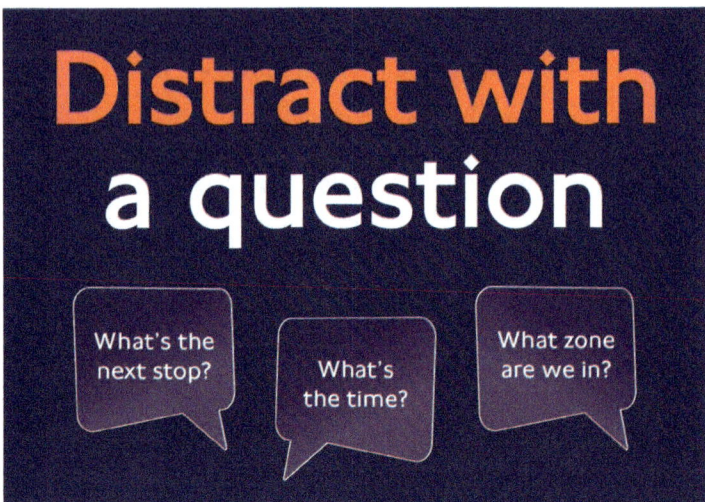

Figure 3.3 - Distract With A Question
Source: TfL 2023 Poster Campaign

THE ROLE OF HR

> *"It's really sad that victims can't speak out and the impact this has on their mental health. The trouble is that organisations are afraid of being sued, so they go into 'risk management' mode rather than 'caring for the employee' mode"*

Many women do not report their experiences through the official work channels, typically because they doubt they will be believed.

> *"A very senior male colleague harassed me. A group of us got in a taxi together and he followed me home. He was a lot older and I think he was in love with me. I didn't tell anyone because I didn't think anyone would believe me. He was well-respected"*

And too often when they are believed, the response is unsatisfactory.

> *"A male colleague, 10 years older, showed me a lot of interest and was very open about how much he liked me. It was very awkward on work trips as we would go to a nice restaurant and for cocktails, then he would pay PA[13]. He'd put something in his mouth that looked like Viagra. And it was very difficult in the hotel when we walked past my room. I tried to keep him at bay and began making up reasons not to travel with him. In the end I had to go to HR as he didn't know where to draw the line. But I didn't want to make an official complaint, so I had to deal with it myself, telling him straight that I wasn't going to be his mistress"*

Case Study: False Accusations

I was treated very badly by one individual in an ordeal that lasted eight months. He was 12 years older than me, senior to me until I was promoted above him. I had to make him redundant, and he claimed it was only because he had rejected my sexual advances. He then tried to sue me and to wreck my career.

Before I knew of his accusations, HR asked me to describe his character. I said he had a schoolboy sense of humour: he'd invite me to sit on his knee and once said he'd dreamt of me in a bikini. I always laughed it off as him being a bit of a lad. Then it turned out that he had been making notes about me for two years and filing them in his 'Protect My Arse' folder, embellishing what I had actually said for effect. Once after COVID our stuff had been moved out of our lockers into a shared area, and he'd recorded me as saying: "*Imagine if I'd had my dildo in there!*" This was a complete fabrication.

When he realised his claim had no grounds and would not be successful, he switched to age and sex discrimination. Then he dropped the case on the day of the tribunal, in exchange for a reference.

The whole thing has changed my behaviour and my identity. I am so much less trusting and I now dress incredibly conservatively – I don't want to ever open myself up to such accusations again.

It happened 14 months ago and I'm still working through it.

---

13   on his personal account, not charging it as a business expense

Similar to TfL's approach, shifting the culture to one which normalises reporting and which has a minimum standard of HR response could make all the difference. Victims might then feel that it's worth the stress and embarrassment of reporting what they have experienced.

And maybe a bolder, more sustainable solution is for organisations to shift their HR perspective, pivoting from *'protect the business from being sued'* to *'do the right thing for the employee'*. Often people resort to aggressive legal action because they are aggrieved that they have not been listened to or treated with respect. Perhaps the loyalty generated from the sensitive handling of upsetting complaints would more than negate this risk.

In the Sheep Shack

4. THE MOTHERHOOD PENALTY

4.1 SUMMARY

1. It is very difficult for women to have it all! Most women perceive that their decision to have children has impeded their career progression

2. For this to change, we need equality at home, with men and women sharing childcare and domestic responsibilities equally and taking equal lengths of parental leave

3. Great maternity policies extend beyond maternity pay and time off for antenatal appointments. There should be heightened awareness of the challenges around fertility including miscarriage and IVF, both of which typically happen in secrecy and can be emotionally and physically devastating

4. Returning mothers often experience guilt and separation anxiety at a time when they are trying to readjust to being back at work. Employers can help ease the transition back with a well-structured keeping in touch programme and a maternity coach but, more simply, through managers acting with sensitivity and kindness

5. Allowing flexibility in working hours is hugely helpful to working mothers and can make all the difference in keeping them in the business. It also enables working fathers to lean in and share domestic responsibilities

4.2 THE MYTH OF HAVING IT ALL

> *"I was sold the pup. I was Thatcher's child - propelled and compelled to be exceptional in my career. I was told to take advantage of being smart, that it was my opportunity. But who was the clever one? I've taken on the big role. I now have to juggle all the time. Am I actually the winner or the loser? Don't kid yourself: you cannot have it all!"*

In the 1990s, Nicola Horlick was making front page news. A hugely successful fund manager, she conquered the corporate ladder, achieved fame and fortune AND produced six children. The tabloids crowned her 'Superwoman'. She was the shining example of how women could, in fact, have it all. Although Horlick herself noted: *"It's ridiculous that I am known as 'superwoman'... Look at someone who has no help at home and holds down a job. Or look at me with my nanny and my secretary. Who would you call 'superwoman'?"*[14]

> *"When you have kids, you have to write off five years"*

> *"So many younger women don't want kids. They see the rat-race struggle and it looks shit. And they ask me what I did at the weekend: I went to a kids' party; they went out for a bottomless brunch"*

> *"When it goes well, I feel like superwoman. But it's a knife edge. All it takes is a sick child and then it goes wrong"*

14 'The Human Face of Nicola Horlick" - Emma Clark, BBC News, 19th December 2002

> *"My decision to have children created so much work. Even though I had a full-time nanny, the burden fell on me. I wanted to balance being a good mum, and that led me to step off the executive corporate ladder. I just couldn't work all the time"*

EQUALITY BEGINS AT HOME

> *"I didn't have children by choice. As a 9-year-old, I had to change the nappies of my youngest siblings. I just equated children with housework, growing up seeing the women in the kitchen and the men down the pub. It's not a fair divvying up of responsibilities - children are an impediment to your freedom and options"*

If women can't get equality at home, can they expect it at work? Is inequality a learned response or is it conditioned, ingrained every time the woman reloads the dishwasher and doesn't let the man hold the baby? There is still a societal expectation that women run the home and, whilst that persists, we perpetuate the expectation that the woman is the primary carer. Fathers at work are lauded if they make the occasional effort, when a mother is condemned for not prioritising her work. We don't see the inequality.

> *"I was fortunate that I had a deal with my husband that one of us would always be within 15 minutes of the children. But it impacted me more as I was seen as the primary carer"*

To make it work, we need help. That comes in many guises - a partner, a nanny, a mums' network, extended family. But we do need it. We're not going to win any medals trying to do it on our own.

> *"If you want a permanent relationship with children involved, you need to choose the right man"*

70

> *"If you don't have a good husband, you need*
> *to find other support at home"*

Whilst women can be very helpful to each other, they can also judge each other with harsh suspicion, particularly around parenting where there is a natural defensiveness about the compromises in one's own choice. This is apparent at the school gates, where there is a palpable pecking order.

The full-time mums sit at the top of the tree, the heart and soul of the school. They run the PTA and the second-hand school uniform sales; the school fête and the nativity costumes wouldn't happen without them. But at what cost? Many have given up an independent income and persona to be 'Mum' and hide their insecurities under a cloak of superiority. Threatened that their husbands, on whom they now so utterly depend, are spending their days in the company of these women with their smart clothes and smart opinions, they mask their fear behind disdain, looking down on the working mums' lack of commitment to the school, scorning their freeloading.

And the working mums don't need much nudging to feel that they are failing; from scraping the sleep dust out of their child's eyes so they won't both have to stay at home because of conjunctivitis, to forgetting it's *'Come as your favourite book character'* day. Everything is a rush, a juggle, laser-focused at the office until the phone goes and the worry flashes that it's the school and something has gone wrong.

> *"I was trailblazing, working three days a week, with a very*
> *high public profile. There were no women on the board*
> *and I could have put myself forward, but I didn't want to*
> *swap spending time with the children for regular European*
> *flights with my male colleagues who were all bullies"*

> *"For some roles, it may just not be possible to do the job well and have a family. When client demands are 24/7 the sad answer is: it's not. We respond to everything instantly, which is not compatible with a family. When the partners go on holiday, we put our kids in the kids' clubs and just get on with our work. It is traditional and old-fashioned, and women still need to behave like men in order to progress"*

And it is important for society that we get it right. Because working mothers, at their best, when the support mechanisms are in place, are unstoppable.

> *"Working parents will be the most productive people on your team. They are highly incentivised to produce results the fastest. When a team member becomes a parent, it's not an inconvenience or cost to the team. It's a gift - provided they are supported accordingly"*

To eliminate the career penalty of having children, men and women need to take equal periods of parental leave.

4.3 PREGNANCY

> *"I joined my new company mid-career and then found out I had to be there three years to get more than SMP[15]"*

The highs and lows of pregnancy can be mind-altering, life changing. And many women live through them at the office, keeping their hopes and fears under wraps, not wanting to let colleagues know of their plans to reproduce because of the inherent career risk.

---

15   The UK's Statutory Maternity Pay. In 2024, it was 90% of average weekly earnings for the first 6 weeks, then the lower of 90% of average weekly earnings or £184.03 for the next 33 weeks

Many businesses have supportive policies to smooth their employees through the maternity process. But many do not, failing to attach sufficient value to the loyalty generated by looking after employees when they are at their most vulnerable, not appreciating the irreparable damage that treating them badly can cause.

> *"The day I was going on maternity leave I was called into my boss's office. He told me that they were changing the maternity policy and I would no longer receive my commission payments. This was a huge amount of money and targeted only at me, as the sole woman of childbearing age eligible to receive commissions. I challenged the decision and they backed down, but I was 38 weeks pregnant and had to be rushed to hospital with pre-eclampsia symptoms brought on by the stress of it all. I decided at that point I would not be returning to work there"*

> *"I had an ectopic pregnancy. They have a 1 in 100 occurrence and can be fatal. Sometimes you can't see where the embryo had embedded, so the treatment varies from an operation, to chemotherapy, to waiting to see if it is reabsorbed. It was really difficult for about six weeks, as I was on alert for an immediate hospital trip. I didn't tell my manager - he frequently cut me down, stole my ideas, yelled at me and lied to me. It really underlined the mismatch in commitment - I gave so much to that business, including risking my health, and my manager just bullied me"*

> *"I had unplanned pregnancies that I terminated. It was very sad. Heartbreaking. I would have loved another child. But there was the cost-of-living crisis, the expense of nursery fees, the impact on my career, plus I couldn't afford to be out for nine months - only six months on full pay, three on half. I had overwhelming guilt, on top of my hormones being in turmoil. I told my female boss who was very supportive and had had an abortion too. But I know what my role was like - if I wasn't there to do the work, someone else would quickly fill my shoes"*

> *"There is a false narrative that you can have kids whenever you like. I'm super-sensitive to talking about my issues with young kids, in case there are people around me who are struggling to get pregnant"*

Being pregnant at work is one thing, but juggling the process of getting pregnant with working can be very challenging.

> *"I'd just started a new job, cycling in and breastfeeding my 11-month-old baby. I was tired all the time. One day I was giving a presentation and I felt something move inside me. I bought a pregnancy test and it was positive. I was stunned. It was virtually impossible for me to be pregnant, as I'd had postpartum issues that made sex incredibly painful. I took two more tests, both positive, so I booked an emergency scan. I was 21 weeks and three days pregnant - my first baby had been huge and I'd thought that was why my stomach was still large. I told one of my colleagues and he quoted a John Lennon song: 'Life is what happens to you while you're busy making other plans'"*

> *"I had been trying to get pregnant for five years and had stalled changing jobs because I was trying for a baby. Eventually I decided to change jobs anyway and by the time I started, I was pregnant. It felt inappropriate, like people were judging me for starting a new job and immediately getting pregnant. As if I'd planned it. One colleague was pissed off because she had been delaying trying for her second baby because of the new boss coming in - me"*

The World Health Organisation estimates that one in six people are affected by infertility.

During 2021 in the UK, 55,000 women had 76,000 IVF cycles, with an overall success rate of 27%. Success is very age-dependant, ranging from 37% for the under 35s to just 17% for those aged 40-42[16].

Despite such daunting odds, for many couples desperate for their own biological child, IVF represents their last hope. But it is an expensive and gruelling process. It is very challenging to navigate the rollercoaster of medical procedures and emotions whilst working. But many, many women do. And most of them do it in secret.

> *"Before IVF, we were trying to get pregnant. After another failed attempt, a friend sent me some balloons at work to cheer me up. Someone saw them and posted on a work group chat: 'Have you seen the balloons? Maybe we'll hear the patter of tiny feet soon?'. And my boss came into my office, saying: 'You will tell me when you're pregnant, won't you?'. I went to the toilet and cried. I realised work was going to be much harder"*

---

16   Source: The Human Fertilisation and Embryology Authority

Case Study: The IVF Rollercoaster

I was very lucky to already be a partner when I had my IVF, so I had a lot of independence and autonomy. I needed it, as the process was gruelling.

I had six rounds of IVF, each cycle lasting two months. The first stage lasts a month and they take your hormones to ground zero. You feel terrible. Then they inject a cocktail of high levels of hormones into your stomach every day for about three weeks to induce your follicles to ripen, ideally around 20 rather than just the one you get in your natural monthly cycle. Twice, I was overstimulated. Then you have daily blood tests and a scan every other day for another three weeks. I worked from the London office and moved into a studio flat nearby for that period so I could be close to the hospital. I had to drink gallons of milk and water to save my kidneys - I was weeing every 10 minutes.

Then I had a small operation to harvest the eggs. It you're lucky, they take about 20, of which they might fertilise 15 and 5 might be viable. I had two put in each time and then you have the stress of a two-week window to see if they embed.

I felt desperate each time it failed, emotionally devastated, like I would never, ever have children. Then they gave me extra drugs as they thought my immune system was killing off the embryos, which meant a regular infusion and having to inject myself in the buttocks every day.

It took four years to get pregnant. My twins were born premature via c-section and I was feeding and changing them every 3.5 hours through the night. Then my husband and I split up when they were four. But I've no regrets, although it has been an absolute challenge, like climbing Everest every day.

Case Study: How Are Your Children?

I wanted children but I wasn't able to have them. Three times I've been asked by work colleagues: *"How are your children?"*. Someone even claimed to know two of them, telling me their ages. It might have been because I worked part-time and I am caring and nurturing. But it ruined my day, it affected my ability to focus. And it added to my disconnect - this was someone I'd worked with for five years. I'd been feeling invalidated by society for my childlessness and now the same thing was happening at work.

Another time we were out for work drinks. I don't drink. A colleague noticed and asked: *"Have you got something to tell us?"* If I say I've got some news, people assume it's that I'm pregnant. There are a LOT of baby showers. I find it very difficult. There is no celebration of other life events, like going travelling.

It's about having respect. Don't assume that people work part-time because they have kids. Managers with pastoral responsibilities should know how to have these conversations to raise awareness.

"I had endometriosis and was trying to have a baby. There were lots of interventions: mini surgery, D&Cs, IVF drugs that make you difficult to work with. It was a mental rollercoaster. I was in the office, but not firing on all cylinders. Work let me have loads of time off, but they delayed me being made a partner by two years. It was the right decision; I was not a safe pair of hands. I don't regret it - being a mum was more important. But my husband was going through the same thing as me mentally and it didn't slow his career down"

There is a similar shroud of silence surrounding early pregnancy. Women are encouraged not to tell anyone for the first 12 weeks, in case they lose the baby. Perhaps this advice comes from a good place: that it would be upsetting to have to tell everyone you're not pregnant after all. Or perhaps it is because there is some misogynistic shame attached to miscarrying, a failure of one's womanly duty to carry a pregnancy to term.

> *"I found producing children particularly challenging. It was hard to get pregnant and then I had a miscarriage when I was consulting, on a day rate. I couldn't tell anyone why I had to take time off"*

> *"I really struggled with fertility. I had eight miscarriages in total, a lot of them before my first child. I was very open about it. I'd go in and say I was feeling bad, and work was fine about it.*
>
> *In the end I had to have an operation which allowed me to get pregnant. When I did, people told me: 'You're not supposed to tell anyone before 12 weeks.' I thought about why that is. And there is a double taboo around it: will I lose the baby, and will I lose my promotion prospects? We need to make it OK to talk about our fertility journeys and let people celebrate a happy moment"*

Yet miscarriages are very common[17], affecting one in five women. In the UK, 15% of all pregnancies end in miscarriage, equating to around 250,000 pregnancies each year. Little surprise then that a lot of them happen at work.

---

17 Source: Sands and Tommy's Joint Policy Unit, based on 2021-22 NHS data, UK Government response to the Pregnancy Loss Review, July 2023

> *"I have had some internal training on diversity, menopause etc, but it's a bit staccato unless you live and breathe it every day. Three members of staff had miscarriages and I found it easier to relate to, as my wife had had a miscarriage. I really understood this was a difficult thing for them to tell me about and, even in those cases when it doesn't have a huge physical implication, it can be much bigger psychologically and not a thing you just draw a nice, neat line around and say it's over in two weeks. I also understood that it's different if it's the first miscarriage, or one between babies"*

> *"I had a miscarriage with an unplanned pregnancy and the doctor told me I could take up to two weeks off. But I wanted to go back for the distraction. Plus it was nobody's business - I worked for a small company and I was worried that if they found out, they would think I was trying for a family. I debated with myself whether I should be telling them so that we could collectively prepare. But then if I didn't get pregnant successfully, would that mean I was risking my career? And is it weird to be that transparent?"*

> *"I went for a scan at 8 weeks and there was no heartbeat. They told me to leave it for a week and then to come back in for a D&C. I remember saying to myself: 'I can't do it on this day, because I have a client meeting.' Then I recognised that I might think I'm important, but everyone can else can manage without me. But I only took two days off, then I wanted to be back into it"*

Workplaces could really help women by changing the narrative about miscarriage, raising awareness and providing support so that women do not have to suffer the wretched indignity of bleeding in the toilets, in secret, alone. Trying to choke back their sobs as they clean themselves up, walk back to their desk and get on with the workday until they can go to hospital.

4.4 BACK TO WORK

> *"I was going for job interviews with a three-month-old. I was wearing a trouser suit - the only suit I could fit into post pregnancy - and was told by a female recruitment consultant that I looked scruffy. And then people assumed that because I had one child, I'd have a second"*

GUILTY MUM SYNDROME

Some women have a financial set-up that allows them to choose whether to return to work. But many women don't have that luxury. Either way - through choice or necessity - there are decisions to be made about childcare and these bring huge financial, logistical and emotional challenges.

Leaving a child for the first time can be an enormous wrench - after all, as a species we are hard-wired to protect our offspring - so going back to work can feel like abandonment. It can also feel incredibly liberating after months of existing in a tedium of baby classes, nappies, food puréeing and posset-proof clothing. Suddenly, we get to play at being a grown-up again, wearing smart clothes, with time for coffees, concentration and conversations that don't revolve around motherhood. But we are damned either way, as both tap into our endless capacity for maternal guilt, as well as magnifying our imposter syndrome.

> *"I've always suffered from Guilty Mum Syndrome. My advice? Don't! Your kids will thank you for being ambitious"*

To quash these feelings, women often feel they have to prove themselves on both home and work fronts. This can lead to exhaustion, at a time when they are often still recovering from pregnancy and, for the 1 in 6 women it affects, post-natal depression[18]. It's not helped by crass comments, often levelled by unsympathetic male colleagues with stay-at-home wives.

> *"Why are you back? You should be at home looking after your children"*

> *"Is your husband OK with you going back to work after you've had a baby?"*

EASING THE TRANSITION

Some businesses do a grand job in smoothing the transition back, with the best ones organising regular 'Keeping In Touch' days during maternity leave and offering the services of a maternity coach. Done well, these can be really helpful; done badly, they can create a greater sense of divide and alienation than they solve.

> *"I had two periods of maternity leave. Financially, the company was very generous, but during the first period, my manager didn't really engage. Any discussions were around the practicalities: bonus, accrued holiday, form-filling. But a good and generous parental policy isn't the end of the story - there's much more to it than that. It's about thinking ahead to how they can make the returning process easy: providing regular, structured email updates (and checking whether to do so via your personal or work email address) and Keeping In Touch days"*

---

18   15-20% of women experience depression and anxiety in the first year after birth - NICE 2023

> *"I kept my first maternity leave really short and went in for a Keeping in Touch day. I was still breast feeding so I'd had to pump in advance and I'd arranged for my mum to come down to look after the baby. My boss cancelled twice. He had no conception of the logistics and planning involved, what it takes to come in for the day"*

> *"I was told by my maternity coach to keep it quiet that I was coming back four days a week"*

Good policies are fundamental, but sometimes kindness and understanding from an empathetic boss or colleague is all that is needed. And people who get that it's not all a bed of roses, something that can be difficult to admit to when it is contrary to societal expectation, and potentially insensitive to those who are struggling to have a family.

> *"We are told that pregnancy and motherhood are a magical experience. But what about when they're not? There can be a backlash if you complain about pregnancy issues, or worrying about how it will impact your career. You're not allowed to say that out loud. It's disrespectful to those with fertility issues. And you can be told 'But it was your choice to have a family'"*

> *"When I came back from my first maternity leave, I was exhausted: my son didn't sleep for 14 months, and I went back when he was 10 months old. I had a very supportive male boss with a stay-at-home wife. He transposed his own experience and talked to me to about it, saying: 'Let's go and get a coffee'. He tried. But I was allowed to work from home for one day, and he'd assumed my child would be with me when, of course, I had childcare arranged. He'd assumed I wouldn't actually be working"*

And the situation requires even greater sensitivity for single mothers.

> "Bringing up children as a single parent is a full-time job in itself. A couple of the senior partners I work with don't know how to use the washing machine. I do three loads a day. I look at what I've had to do just to get out the door. The mountain of hidden, additional indirect challenges that I have to overcome just to be able to compete. It's not a level playing field"

> "In many law firms, you are entitled to a one-month sabbatical after ten years. The men get to go on amazing trips: Bolivia, Chile. My female colleagues don't. One used hers to help her teenagers through their GCSEs. I'm using mine as summer holiday cover to look after my kids"

> "When I had my baby, I didn't want to tell work that I was bringing him up on my own. So I over-compensated, working longer hours. I had to go on a business trip whilst I was still breastfeeding, so I took my 10-month-old son and nanny with me on the flight with all male colleagues. I didn't tell anyone that they were travelling with me - it felt like a walk of shame. Part of it was my perception, my bias. Only now am I comfortable with it. I shouldn't have had to do it with guilt. It was impressive and I should have held my head high"

However, for some women the experience of motherhood can also be very empowering. It reveals inner strengths which can translate into renewed self-belief at work.

> "Until recently, I was the reliable multi-tasker who got stuff done. Now I'm Head of Business Development. I only had the confidence to do this after I became a mother. I felt much more powerful - if I could give birth and look after two kids, I could do anything. I had gravitas, was better able to set boundaries, took less crap, was ready to take more risks"

Many women come back after maternity leave to find their job isn't quite what it was when they left it.

> *"When I was on maternity leave, they assumed I wouldn't come back. When I did, they had employed two people to do my job, so they assigned me to something else that was a lot less interesting. I didn't challenge it because I'd lost a lot of confidence being off for nine months. Everyone assumes you're the same person, but you're really not"*

> *"I took a planned one-year career break, but then COVID happened and it turned into three years so that I could home-school my six- and nine-year-old children. I came back into a pro women environment, with plenty of programmes to get you back into work. But there was a lack of look-back at skills and I had to prove myself as they see a woman and a mother first, not a CFO. It took me a long time to get a job, and I had to accept a one-third reduction to my previous salary. They felt they were taking a risk hiring me"*

And in the worst instances, they find themselves in a hostile environment where they have been set up to fail.

Case Study: Set Up To Fail

I came back from my first maternity leave early, after six months rather than nine. I was a trader, but they had no desk for me, no phone, no computer. For three months, I had nothing to do. My colleagues were told not to speak to me and HR said they didn't care.

Finally, a senior person realised there was a problem and then, three days later, my boss told me I could have my job back. But he was angry about it and told me I was never to put him in that position again. He was six foot two and we were standing in a small room with a photocopier, him holding a pair of scissors. It felt threatening.

They found a guy to share his trading book with me, telling him it was a risk and if I messed up, he would lose his job too.

Then they tried to sabotage me. When I went to the toilet, they modified the pricer on my spreadsheet, got their friend at a hedge fund to ask me for a price, and then reported me when I quoted the wrong price, requesting a formal inspection as if I were a rogue trader. Fortunately for me, there were witnesses.

I then moved to a different country with the same firm and they gave me a shit book, with no potential to make money, no clients. But my boss was brilliant, telling me he didn't care about my gender, he just needed me not to leave at 4pm and to make money. And I did. I flew. I mastered it. And I caught up on pay and on promotion.

WORK/LIFE BALANCE

"Having senior men working part time makes a big difference"

"At my company, all the mums were part-time, typically four days a week. I felt pressure to do the same"

> *"We are not creative about how we charge for our time. Every six minutes is accounted for. If I don't work on a Friday, I lose all those six minute blocks and have to take a 20% pay cut, rather than being judged on what I am achieving and how productive I am in the four days I do work. I asked the business to look at the money my team brings in. If it's the same, then pay me the same. The quid pro quo is that, because I'm paid full time, I'm compared with the full-time peer group when determining my share of the annual profits. I'm happy with that"*

COVID and the acceptance of hybrid working that it heralded has been transformative in allowing women flexibility to manage their work/life balance without stigma. But for those that want a more formal work/life balance demarcation, it is still hard to be taken seriously and for it not to affect your career prospects.

These pressures of achieving a balance are reflected in the demographic of executive MBA programs, a useful career advancement pathway for mid-career professionals. Typically in their early 30s to early 40s, only 37%[19] are women. Perhaps not surprising, given that studying needs to be done in the evenings and at weekends, hardly compatible with family life.

> *"I've leant out as I've got older. Advancement used to be really important to me, but now I find I'm not putting my hand up for director roles. I have a sharp-elbowed junior colleague, and I just don't have that fight left in me. It's seen as a negative that I do an extra day at home, and I've been told I can't go down the man-management route as I need to leave at 4:30pm. Our business has grown through PE investment and we have to showcase growth. There are a few senior women and three female directors, but none of them has young kids"*

---

19   Source: QS Business School Survey 2022

"I came back to work on four days a week after my first child. After my second, I was told I would have to go back to five days if I wanted to get promoted"

"Having a family is what has held me back in my career. But I wasn't hindered by the organisations I worked for, but by my experience of juggling being a mum, because I didn't want to miss out on the kids. The CFO would often say: 'Let's come back to this at 6pm', but I worked flexibly part time. Even though I had a supportive husband, I hindered myself with two major responsibilities - my job and my children"

"When I started out, there were two strong female managers in their 50s who were really supportive. But I found I had to take roles which allowed me to leave at 4:30pm to do the school pick-up, or that allowed me to be flexible in case the children were ill. You are seen as being less reliable when you have a young child. And if you are in 8:30am to 4:30pm, you can't win against 8am-7pm male presenteeism"

Case Study: Breaking Point

I'm respected now, but I once worked in a team of six and I was the only female. Two of us were in our late 30s and the other four were in their 50s, all with wives who worked part-time or were semi-retired. The manager often singled me out and patronised me: "You don't need to worry yourself with that.' I felt very micromanaged, constantly checked in on, and he didn't do that with the others. I'd challenge it, but it made no difference.

He was aware that I had three children (twin girls, and a son with the cognitive awareness of a 2-year-old) and a husband who worked away. I had to leave 'early' at 5pm, and he'd say: *"XX needs to go now, but we'll carry on without her"*, or point out that someone else had to pick up the project.

It had been simmering, then after a week of him constantly checking in on me, demanding to know where I'd been when I was working from home and he couldn't get hold of me instantly (I'd been in the kitchen getting something to eat), he called me on my laptop at 5:30pm. He could see I was in the kitchen, managing three kids, food on the hob. He'd made some edits to a report and he wanted me to type them in, even though it would have been quicker to do it himself. I was at breaking point. I said no and ended the call.

The next morning, I had an epiphany. I decided not to log on. I called HR, said I wanted a few days. I got signed off for two weeks with stress and I never went back. I told HR about some of the comments and how I was treated. But he's still there.

5. 'WOMEN'S PROBLEMS'

5.1 SUMMARY

1. Women's hormones fluctuate much more than men's, a cyclicality that is much less suited to conventional working patterns. Flexible working schedules alleviate the issue

2. Employers can provide a low cost/high value impact by making sanitary products, disposable knickers and long black cardigans available in toilets, saving embarrassment when periods arrive unexpectedly

3. Menopause affects all women and can cause brain fog and other side effects so severe that women choose to exit the workplace altogether. Being empathetic, destigmatising through education, providing flexible working and being sensitive to the room temperature all help

4. Workplaces providing private medical insurance should check to ensure that menopause-related conditions are not excluded from cover

5. The incidence of cancer for pre-retirement women is statistically higher than for men, often striking as women are clawing back their position on the career ladder following maternity leave. Cancer can have a particularly devastating impact on self-image and self-confidence, with harsher treatments inducing early menopause

5.2 HORMONES

Our productivity levels are affected by how well and how energised we feel. And our hormones play an important part in this. Pre-menopausal women's hormone levels vary significantly more than their male counterparts (Figure 5.1), exhibiting not only monthly but intra-day cyclicality.

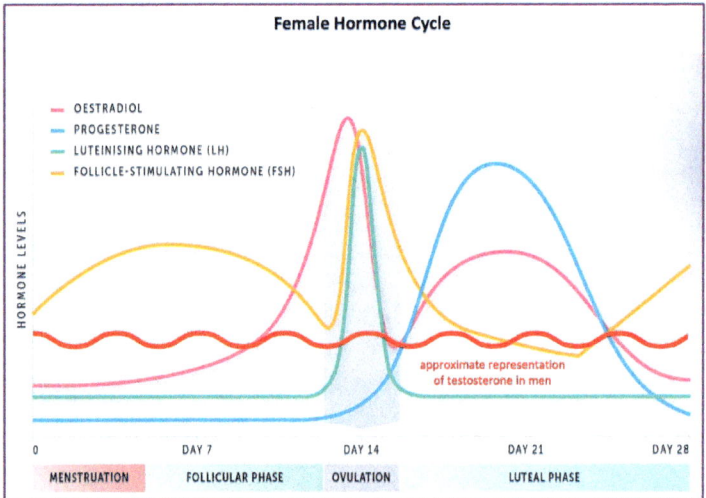

*Figure 5.1 - Female Hormone Cycle\
Source: www.forthwithlife.co.uk*

This presents a problem for women in a conventional work set-up where productivity is generally measured in hours per day or per week, assuming that working capabilities are broadly uniform throughout the year and that everyone will operate at a broadly similar level on any given day. This is not the case for women, where there is a correlation between heightened productivity and oestrogen levels.

A simple counter to this is to reframe employment contracts so that they specify hours per month, rather than per day or per week. This simultaneously de-stigmatises and normalises the issue, and is an easy way to build in flexibility to reflect the natural fluctuations of hormone levels.

PERIODS

For most pre-menopausal women, their monthly cycle is an inconvenience, the pain, bleeding and mood swings a manageable annoyance. However, when your cycle is irregular, periods can be a source of intense shame and embarrassment. Employers can really help out here, making a low cost difference that has a high value impact in a moment of need. All toilets provide toilet paper, but not all provide sanitary products. Making these available in work toilets, together with disposable knickers for when a period starts unexpectedly, is incredibly thoughtful and can feel like a lifeline. Some establishments even have a supply of long black cardigans hanging in the toilet cubicles for loan to save embarrassment in case of extensive leaks.

> *"I remember bleeding horribly at work once and having to go out pant-less to buy new ones, my jacket tied round my waist to conceal the blood stains"*

> *"Unisex toilets at work are really uncomfortable. I don't like sharing facilities. Having your period and the toilet doesn't flush and there's a man waiting to use the cubicle after you"*

ENDOMETRIOSIS

But for some women, heavy periods and endometriosis have a very severe health impact, all the more challenging because of their regular recurrence. Endometriosis affects roughly 10%[20] of pre-menopausal women.

---

20 Source: World Health Organisation

This can significantly impinge one's ability to work, and businesses should be alert to the additional support that those suffering may require.

5.3 MENOPAUSE

"HRT has saved me.
It helps me to sleep, to function, to manage my moods and anxiety. It allows me to compete on a level playing field"

Menopause is something that half the population will experience. Whilst some women breeze through it, many do not. Some struggle to such an extent that they end up leaving the workforce permanently, resulting in a detrimental loss of experience, diversity and wisdom.

Best-in-class workplaces recognise this and are thinking carefully how they can support women through a life phase that has physical, mental and emotional side effects, some of them very long-lasting. The starting point is acknowledging this as an area where women may need help, then raising awareness through education and offering resources that managers can harness so they can better understand the implications and the optimal response.

> *"We're not engaged with menopause policy - it marks your card. I work in HR and I've seen some of the outcomes"*

> *"I can see why women drop out of the workplace after menopause. My colleagues don't realise I'm struggling. It has really affected my mental health. We've run wellness sessions at work about it, and are trying to normalise talking about it"*

Encouraging regular breaks and allowing more flexible working are easy ways to help manage the tiredness and brain fog. Discussing menopause so it is normalised helps to remove the stigma of a hot flush. Issuing small desk, or hand-held, fans as standard is a thoughtful touch.

> *"When I went through the menopause, I had terrible brain fog. My contract allowed me to work from home one day a week, but I had a new boss and she didn't like it. She would regularly put meetings in my diary for that day and insist I come in for them. I would sit in a booth pretending to read a newspaper, hiding, until my brain could function again"*

> *"Women often won't speak up when they're physically
> uncomfortable, and male colleagues should be conscious
> of this. It's a courtesy. For menopausal colleagues, be really
> aware about the room temperature. Factor in regular breaks
> in case women are on their period or they are pregnant. Don't
> assume we're all going to tough it out. It's not a bike race"*

Businesses that offer private medical care should check whether menopause is covered. Healthcare providers do offer menopause cover, but generally it's an elected add-on. Given that all women experience menopause and are likely to benefit from peri-menopausal testing and speedy access to HRT, there is a strong case for it to be part of standard cover.

> *"Female health is a matter of empathy. I found out my baby
> was at high risk of Down's Syndrome and I got pneumonia. It
> made all the difference when I was told: 'You're not going to do
> that, you need to go home and sort it!' I was given permission"*

5.4 THE NOT-SO-RANDOM ASSASSIN

Until we understand more about its causes, cancer strikes as a random assassin, causing devastation in its wake and lasting psychological damage, even for those who survive. As many of us know from first-hand experience, managing a cancer diagnosis - even when the prognosis is good - is a devastating, gruelling process.

As well as the physical toll of the treatment, which is profound if you go through chemotherapy, there is the mental anguish of coming to terms with your mortality, and the organisational nightmare of managing a riot of hospital appointments. All of these play havoc with your working life.

Statistically though, it does not attack males and females in a similar pattern, with significantly higher incidence rates for females in the under 60s age groups and significantly lower rates in the older age groups (Figure 5.2).

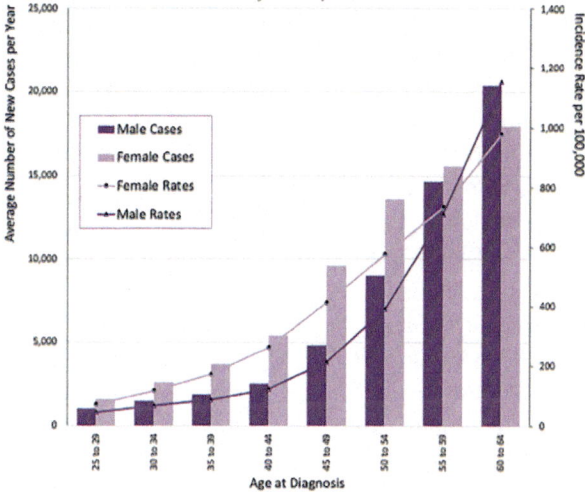

Cancer incidence for women of working age is significantly higher than for men

Cancer Incidence for UK Population 2016 - 2018

Figure 5.2 - UK Cancer Incidence
Source: Cancer Research UK, 07/24

In other words, women are significantly more likely than men to be struck down by cancer when they are mid-career, often when they are working hard to claw back their position on the career ladder following maternity leave and managing small children.

> "I had my son at 40 and was made redundant when I was pregnant. Then I got breast cancer and was put on Tamoxifen21 for five years. I wasn't ready to be tipped into menopause. It took me seven years to recover"

---

21 a drug to prevent recurrence of oestrogen-linked breast cancers by suppressing oestrogen, inducing menopausal symptoms.

Layer on this that 51% of cancers in the 25-49 age group and 41% in the 50-75 age group are 'female' cancers (Figure 5.3) - although breast cancer can and does affect men too - for which the treatments can have particularly cruel side effects, including loss of fertility, loss of libido, loss of feminine characteristics (hair, breasts), on top of inducing early menopause. The impact of these on self-image and self-confidence cannot be underestimated.

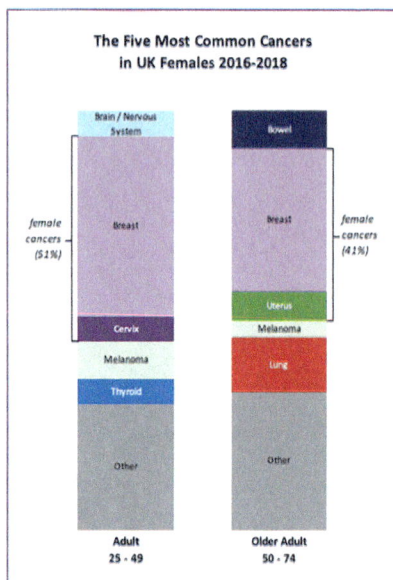

Figure 5.3 - Most Common Female Cancers
Source: Cancer Research UK, 07/24

Armless?

6. AGGRESSIONS - MICRO AND MACRO

6.1 SUMMARY

1. We live in a world designed by men, for men. So much of our everyday existence is gender-biased that we have become blind to it. Particular workplace annoyances are the design of name badges and portable microphones

2. Microaggressions are increasingly recognised and are commonplace. We can achieve a sense of proportion about when to challenge and when to 'smile and wave', using an Intended/Not Intended versus Mild/Egregious framework

3. It is generally women who adopt the unofficial role of 'office mum'. This is a valuable function, making the workplace that much nicer for everyone else, but it is generally looked down on and detracts from their ability to do other work with higher perceived value. The value of the 'office mum' should be officially recognised

4. Networking events generally take place after work, which precludes those with childcare duties from attending. They are also typically centred around events that have greater appeal for men. Offering a range of breakfast, lunch and dinner events and cultural as well as sport options is more inclusive

5. The gender pay gap persists, with too many businesses focusing on narrowing the gap, rather than eliminating it. The cost of losing and replacing disenfranchised females may well outweigh the cost of paying them fairly from the outset

6. Businesses can help combat the glass ceiling effect by enabling them to demonstrate what they can do, recognising they are less likely to speak up or volunteer

7. The glass cliff exists at all levels, as women are seen as willing to roll their sleeves up and are given projects that are fraught with problems

6.2 BY MEN, FOR MEN

In her book 'Invisible Women[22]', Caroline Criado Perez lays bare the ways in which the everyday world has been designed by men, for men, and how this results in shocking inequities. Women are 47% more likely than men to be seriously injured in car crashes, because crash tests are based on male-sized dummies. The average smart phone is too big for the average woman's hand. And women are 50% more likely to be mis-diagnosed if they have a heart attack because we are taught to recognise symptoms that are classically male, whereas women typically present differently.

Another example is in the world of music. There are more women pianists than men in tertiary institutions, and more female than male piano teachers. Yet men dominate at elite levels, winning 82% of 40 major piano competitions[23] , with more than a third featuring all-male finals. Why? It might be because of societal set-up, with men better able to dedicate themselves to the countless hours of practice required. Or inherent misogyny in the music industry, although neither of these explanations is supported by the success of female violinists, who win 75% of competitions. So perhaps it is down to hand size.

Look at the two pianos in Figure 6.1 below. The one on the left is a standard piano, on which I can just about span a nine note stretch. The 7/8ths one on the right was designed specifically for a woman and the keys are marginally narrower; on this, I can comfortably span ten notes. Maybe pianos are just that bit too big for women's hands.

22   'Invisible Women' by Caroline Criado Perez, Vintage, 7th March 2019
23   Source: World Federation of International Music Competitions

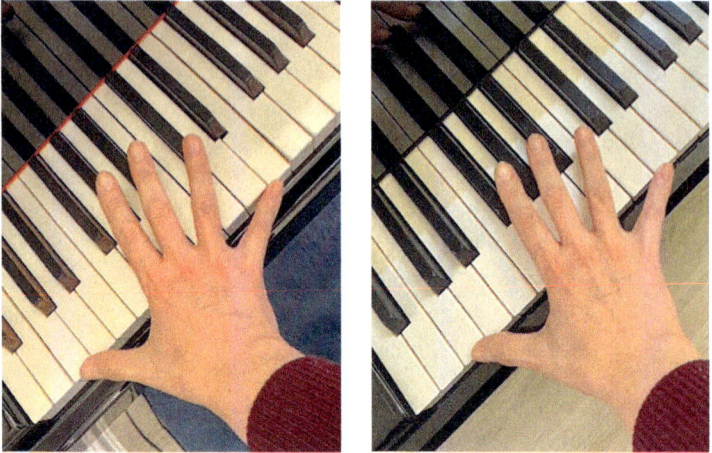

Figure 6.1 - Standard (9 note stretch) & Specialist (10 note stretch) Pianos
Copyright © Jenny Segal 2024

IN THE WORKPLACE

In the workplace, there are so many everyday items that are designed by men, for men that we have become blind to them and accepting of them. Here are a couple of examples.

Women's clothes typically don't have pockets in them. And when they do, they are there for aesthetics rather than practicality, too small to stash anything useful. There are plenty of theories about why this has come to be, many centring around control: if a woman had no means to carry items around secretly, it was much harder for her to act independently and with agency.

One consequence of this persisting fashion inequity is that, when a woman is speaking in public, she has nowhere to put the battery pack that powers her mic. Men can just slip theirs into a jacket pocket or attach it to a trouser belt, whereas women, often belt-less as well as pocketless, have to carry it in their hand.

And at conferences, we are very accustomed to wearing name badges. Most are designed to attach to a jacket lapel (which many women don't have). Or they don't attach without making a hole in your top. Nearly always, they have to be worn on your chest. Why do women have to suffer the indignity of inviting delegates to stare at their breasts to ascertain their name? How would men feel if they were required to wear name badges as codpieces (Figure 6.2)?

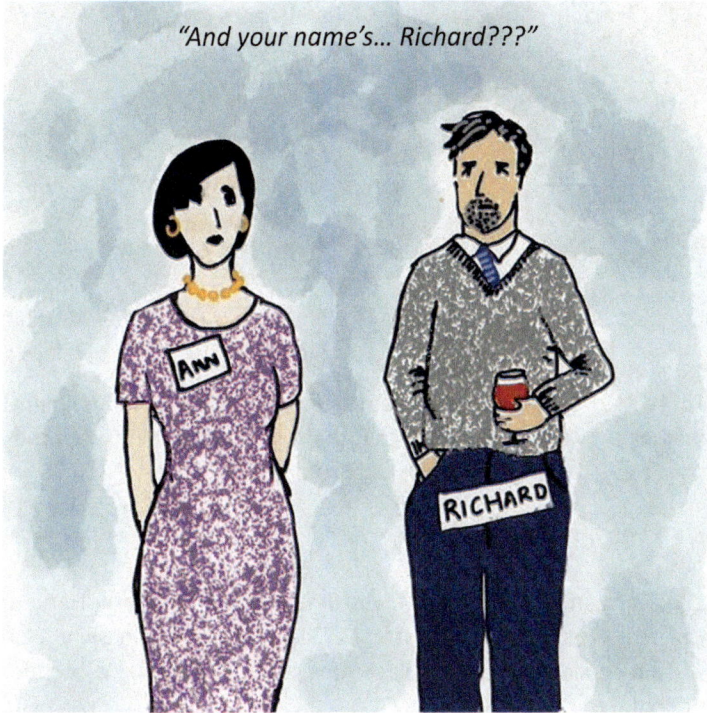

Figure 6.2 - "And Your Name's... Richard???"
Copyright © Jenny Segal & Samantha Oakley

An easy solution is to have a lanyard, like the one in Figure 6.3, which hangs low. It invites a glance well below the breast area and the wearer can raise it to neck height for it to be read easily.

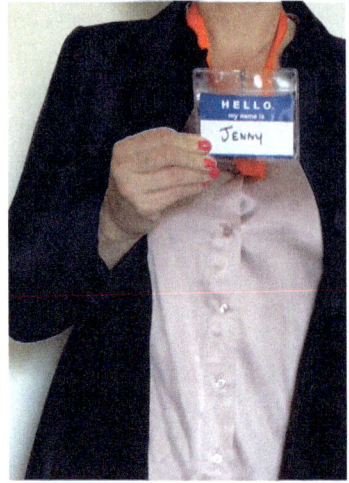

Figure 6.3 - The Perfect Name Badge
Copyright © Jenny Segal 2024

These two examples may seem trivial, but they send subliminal messages to women at work that they are the outsiders. That they have to be the ones who must adapt to fit in.

6.3 MICROAGGRESSIONS

The word "microaggression" was first coined in 1970 by Harvard University psychiatrist Chester M. Pierce to describe slights on African Americans by non-black Americans. It now has a broader definition:

microaggression *noun*:

"a comment or action that subtly and often unconsciously or un-intentionally expresses a prejudiced attitude toward a member of a marginalised group"

– Merriam-Webster Dictionary

and its usage has exploded (Figure 6.4).

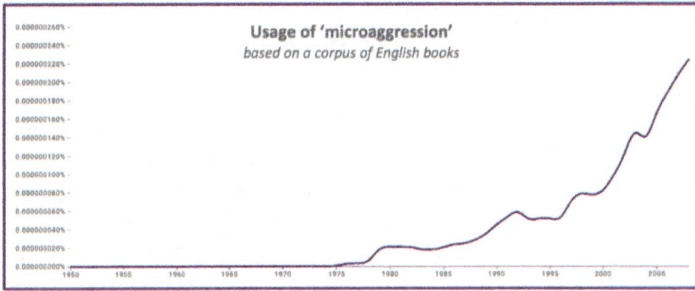

Figure 6.4 - Usage of 'Microaggression'
Source: Google Books Ngram Viewer

When does a microaggression cross the line? In a politically correct world where blatant aggression is not tolerated, a passive-aggressive eye roll or a sigh may be the only outlet we have to vent frustration - does that count? And is a microaggression in the eye of the beholder - what if one person finds it offensive, but the majority of the same marginalised group do not?

> *"People say inept things. How you react to them is your lookout"*

Perhaps we should adopt a framework to classify microaggressions to help us determine when and how to react, where the horizontal axis measures the severity and the vertical measures the intentionality (Figure 6.5).

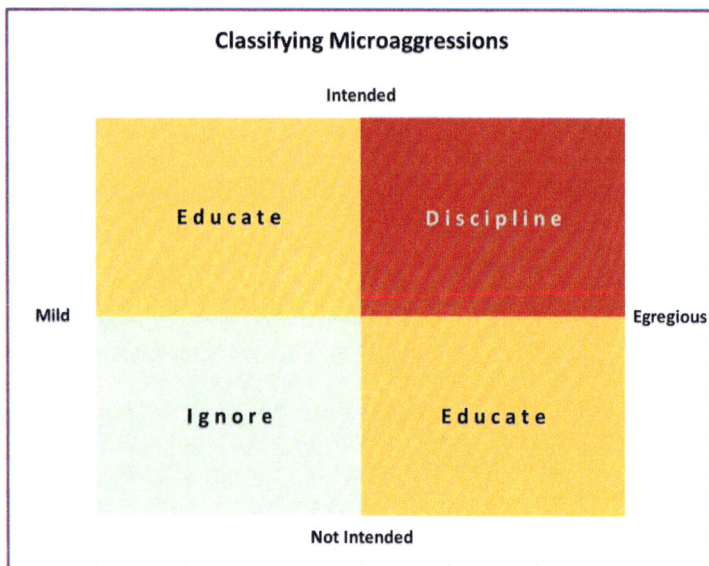

Classifying Microaggressions

Figure 6.5 - Classifying Microaggressions
Copyright © Jenny Segal 2024

Here are some live examples. Which quadrant would you assign each of them to?

> *"A colleague asked for my help with her dissertation. I said: 'Let's meet up in September and if I forget, please remind me.' She took offence, saying she wasn't my secretary. But I would have asked a man the same and as it was me doing her the favour, wasn't it incumbent on her to ensure the meeting happened? But I apologised anyway and said I didn't mean it like that"*

> *"If the boss is away, people ask the first woman they see, rather than the first person that they see, when they'll be back. Ask his assistant or check his diary or send him an email! It's a micro-aggression"*

"I was on the board of a large insurance company and the chair passed over the women, instead appointing two more junior board members as committee chairs. Two women objected, and the chair said to me: 'I hope you're not going to join the witches' coven'"

"Women are the butt of many more micro-aggressions than men. There isn't an equivalent to being told you are upset because you are on your period or you are having a hot flush"

"Said to his (single) PA when she asked to leave early to take her car to be serviced: 'Most people have wives to do that for them'"

"'XXX will know because she loves shopping'. I don't!"

"If you were in a bad mood, you'd had your period. If you were in a good mood, you'd had sex"

"We were discussing 'Love Island' about a very sexual, forward woman. A male colleague in his mid 30s said that she was abusing her sexuality, was very slutty and had obviously slept with loads of men. I argued strongly that she had every right to behave how she wanted with her body, to which he commented: 'No wonder male suicide rates are going up when we have to work with women like you'. No one said anything, including me. I was 26. It's the reason why I now work as a STEM ambassador"

> *"Early in my career, I left a job at a City firm and my boss announced to the team of 20: 'XX is leaving. We're going to replace her with someone better looking'. I was gob-smacked. It didn't affect my confidence; it didn't make me feel like an ugly woman. I just thought, 'What a nob-end'. I told HR and someone else had already reported it. But it didn't make any difference and he continued to have a City career"*

> *"A senior decision-maker at a business partner told me over dinner that our business wouldn't succeed because it had a woman (me) at the helm. He went on and on until I got fed up with him and said: 'If you don't shut up, I'm going to stick my fork in your leg.' It worked - and it inspired me to get into kickboxing to get physically strong so I could knock him to the floor if I needed to. It gave me confidence"*

6.4 'OFFICE MUM'

Women typically fulfil the role of the 'office mum', acting as First Aiders, organising the team nights out, the birthday cards and the Christmas Secret Santa. The stuff that gives the workplace heart and soul and makes it a nicer place for everyone else.

Not only is this additional work that takes additional time, but it has an intrinsic value to the business through the goodwill it generates; happy people are more motivated people and more motivated people produce better work. It also extends to areas with more tangible business benefits, such as team mediation, resolving conflicts, training and mentorship. Either way, the bottom line benefits as a result. But is unrecognised. And hence it is not valued.

> *"More caring and team nurturing energy comes from women than from men. We need to value this consciously. It can be difficult to do this though as we tend to only attach value to things that we do ourselves"*

> *"You are asked to housekeep - to buy the birthday cake, to get the coffee. You have to blink or leave! You have to accept minor infringements. Ask yourself: 'Is it their intention or your interpretation?'"*

Women also tend to take on more than their fair share of low level, administrative work too.

> *"Women join committees to make a difference and get things done. Men join committees to pay lip service. They only come along when the seniors are there, in order to be seen and to look like a good citizen"*

> *"There is a tendency for women to have to roll their sleeves up and sort things out, particularly operational stuff that needs fixing"*

In fact, women may actually be penalised for taking on the role of the office mum. They have to dedicate more of their time to make up for the time that these unofficial mum duties take. And there is a credibility penalty attached to them too - after all, would an important person with important work to do make time for such trivialities?

6.5 GOLF, FOOTBALL OR DRINKS AFTER WORK?

It's not what you know, it's who you know. And to get ahead, you need to know a lot of people; you need to find sponsors and opportunities. And that means networking. Which is difficult to do if you are a working mum with childcare responsibilities.

> *"So many networking events happen in the evenings. The logistics are very hard as my kids have to be picked up at 6pm. There should be a range of options: breakfast, lunch and dinner. It's hampering my career progress"*

And if you do manage to arrange childcare to attend, a lot of the social events themselves appeal to men rather than to women. From golf days to rugby matches, from drinking, to darts and pool. Not many trips to the spa, cream teas or cultural events which are more likely to have a greater draw for women. So when women do arrange their childcare to attend, unlike the men, they are going for the networking benefits, rather than for the joy of the event itself.

Even going for a simple drink with a male colleague or client can present difficulties. There is potential that the invitation might be misconstrued, or that, with the addition of alcohol, the interaction might go dangerously off course. And these concerns can have a detrimental effect on mentorship opportunities, impacting some men's willingness to mentor their female colleagues.

> *"A male colleague told me he never goes out for drinks. That he loves his wife, and he doesn't want to put himself in a position that he might have to apologise for later. I have always managed my male relationships with diligence: I make them more formal, with no banter, and I focus the conversation on their wives"*

6.6 GENDER PAY GAP

> *"You have to make a decision when you have your first child - whether to carry on with your career and rush around, or to take a step back and take on part-time jobs. By your mid 40s, these two paths lead to a marked difference in earnings capacity, so if you end up having marriage difficulties, you are often trapped because you can't afford to leave. You subconsciously make a decision in your early 30s that shapes your whole career and your midlife lifestyle, in a way that doesn't affect men"*

> **Case Study: The Legacy of a 1940s Gender Pay Gap**
>
> Becky lived in an East End council flat in wartime 1940s with her husband and their five children, sewing utility hats for a living. As a piecework machinist, the sum she received per hat was less than the rate paid to her male counterparts. Her husband Bert was unreliable, other than the regularity with which he would start a fight each Friday - payday - so he could storm out and bet his contribution to the housekeeping on the dogs.
>
> But Becky was a proud, determined woman. Over the years, she became friendly with the rent collector who suggested she get the rent book transferred into her name. When there was an opportunity to be rehoused, Becky jumped at it and Bert came home from work to find an empty flat, with no forwarding address.
>
> Her children were all bright, did well in their 11+ entrance exams and got into the local grammar school. Unlike their friends who were forced to leave school at 15 for dead-end jobs to help support their families, Becky aspired for her children to have university educations, a ticket to a better life. One went on to be a doctor, two became dentists and another a very successful banker in The City.

I love this story: Becky was my grandmother and her dentist daughter was my mother. Becky's legacy instilled in me the importance of financial independence and that it is not enough simply to have a career; a professional qualification ensures ongoing employability and saves us from the trap of relying on a partner for financial support.

Whilst the story of Becky seems from another age, the gender pay gap lives on, despite the Equal Pay Act 1970 making it illegal to pay men and women differently for the same work. Since 2017, the UK government has required every company with 250 employees or more to report its gender pay gap data and, in 2024, the disparity had dropped to its lowest level since reporting began. However, women are still being paid just 91p for every £1 a man earns, with the

Construction (22.8%), Finance & Insurance (21.5%), and Education (20%) sectors registering the largest median pay gaps, according to official government data.[24]

> *"I work in HR so I see all the compensation data. My male counterparts earn a lot more than I do and, throughout the whole of the Corporate Services division, the women are consistently the lowest paid. There is no reason for this discrepancy apart from gender bias. The problem is that the women are put into lower compensation bands than their male peers"*

> *"I work in finance and I see all the reward numbers. Our business is full of very talented women and there is a big differential in pay between them and their male colleagues. Closing the gap is seen as the goal. Not eliminating it"*

> *"When I met my husband, we were working at the same company and I was more senior. He was being paid more than me and his bonus was twice mine. You don't find these things out unless you have a conversation"*

Whilst there is societal pressure to eliminate the gender pay gap, aren't businesses incentivised to maintain it? After all, increasing the salaries of their female staff just filters straight through to the bottom line. But the thing is that humans are disincentivised by inequity. Inherently, we value fairness. In psychology circles, this phenomenon has a name, 'disadvantageous-inequity aversion', an instinctual aversion to getting less than others.

It is also prevalent in monkeys and dogs: in an experiment,[25] in exchange for identical tokens one monkey was given a grape whilst

---

24   Source: gov.uk gender pay gap service data as of 5 April 2024

25   Brosnan, S & de Waal, F - Monkeys reject unequal pay. Nature 425, 297–299 (2003)

the other was given cucumber. The money with the cucumber was so enraged it threw the cucumber out of its cage. Whilst underpaid women are less likely to hurl things around, they will be demotivated and may well end up leaving the organisation. Does the cost of reduced productivity from a demotivated employee, or of recruiting and training her replacement (very possibly on a higher salary), make up for the hit of paying her fairly in the first place?

> *"I worked for a woman and she paid my male peer more - I could see as she had the numbers on the desk in front of her. When I challenged her, she told me it was because he was older than me and a guy. As it happens, he had also been done for bullying. I decided we are never having a culture like that here, ever. I'm creating a culture that's fair and equitable"*

6.7 GLASS CEILINGS AND CLIFFS

> *"Women are asked more than men to help out with the operational, administrative tasks. And they are held more accountable than men when things go wrong"*

CEILINGS

What stops women from being promoted as quickly or as far as their male counterparts? Is it simply a consequence of the Motherhood Penalty or is there another dynamic at play?

Case Study: Champagne and Whisky Promotions

I think there are two types of promotion. The champagne promotion is the one you've worked for and, when you get it, you crack open the champagne. But the whisky promotion, that's the one you didn't expect, you didn't feel ready for, where you go and pour yourself a big glass of whisky to steel your nerves.

I've had two internal promotions, both of them whisky. I learnt that you just lean in, even if you don't feel ready or qualified. You just hold your nose and jump. I do ask myself why I didn't get the more orderly champagne promotions. And I think it was because I was working too hard. Women tend to have huge imposter syndrome, so we work really hard to prove to ourselves that we've earned our money. But it's difficult to be strategic when you're so busy.

This is in contrast to our male colleagues who tend to float into promotions because they do less, both in their personal lives and at work where they delegate more. They don't feel the same need to prove themselves.

"Women work hard and they get more stuff done than men. You are valued as a contributor, but it keeps you in your place and you don't get offered the same advancement opportunities as the men when you make yourself indispensable. You don't progress through the stages as easily as a man"

"I used to be a management consultant. Then I saw the quality of the men who were promoted and the quality of women who were not. I decided it was not a game I wanted to play"

To combat the glass ceiling, we need to help women feel that they belong and to bolster their confidence by enabling them to demonstrate what they can do. Women are less likely than men to speak up or volunteer. So we need to tilt the playing field in their favour, proactively creating opportunities for those who are less confident who are, typically, women.

> *"Often, the men in a group want to lead and the women don't. I won't perpetuate that. I pick them out and encourage them to do it, telling them in advance that I'm going to ask them to contribute so that they are prepared. It worked brilliantly with a very quiet, under-confident woman in my team. She did a remarkable job, putting more time into the project and coming up with better ideas. Everyone was blown away by her"*

CLIFFS

The concept of the 'glass cliff', first popularised in 2005, describes the phenomenon whereby women attain the most senior corporate positions at a time when the company is experiencing difficulties, so they are taking on a higher level of risk and they are, almost inevitably, set up to fail. This may be the reason why the average CEO tenure[26] for men is 7.2 years and just 4.5 years for women.

We see the same phenomenon occurring lower down the ranks, with women being given projects to run, or teams to manage, that are fraught with problems.

> *"Every time something was failing, it was given to me. A desk that was unprofitable for years, difficult traders. Successful projects were taken away"*

---

26   average tenure of Fortune 500 CEOS over the past decade as at 2023

"Businesses forgive men who aren't as holistically talented as women. If they cause a problem it will often get hived off and packaged up in a separate role that is then given to a woman as we are good at fixing things, bringing sensitivity and a wider perspective. But these roles can be bit of a poisoned chalice - you're carrying the previous incumbent's baggage, it can tarnish your reputation and then what is your role when you have fixed it? It's the classic glass cliff"

Case Study: The Impossible Task

I think outside the box. I arrived at a financial services company and they tasked me with finding out the names on the committee deciding membership of the Stock Exchange. It's completely secret! They had set me an impossible task. But I was efficient and capable, so I found a way in at the Exchange, and got a meeting in which the guy went on about how bad my firm was. He laughed when I asked who was on the committee, saying he couldn't tell me, but that he would show me on his computer screen. I told my boss, who instructed me to go and have coffees with the names that he didn't know. This kind of thing went on for a few months, them throwing impossible tasks at me. They set a higher bar for me because I was a woman. It stopped once I'd proven I could do it and had gained the trust of the CEO.

Yes, of course I was being targeted. Being a woman puts you under the biggest spotlight. So lean in! Take it as a challenge.

Shadow Birds

7. GUILTY UNTIL PROVEN INNOCENT

7.1 SUMMARY

1. We assume that men know what they're doing until they make a mistake, and that women do not until they prove their worth: men are innocent until proven guilty, whilst women are guilty until they prove themselves to be innocent

2. Imposter Syndrome is more prevalent in women (54%) than in men (38%)

3. Men tend to overestimate their own intelligence, whilst females tend to underestimate theirs

4. A lack of knowledge causes both men and women to overestimate their own competence

5. Taken together, these tendencies can lead men to assume greater authority than is merited

6. 'The Authority Gap' is the phenomenon whereby women are not afforded the authority that their experience and expertise merit. It can result in mansplaining and women being misjudged, spoken over and not listened to and having their ideas stolen

7. When women do have authority, we don't like them displaying alpha male traits. Our perceptions are gender-dependent and behaviours that we praise in a man, we can find uncomfortable in a woman

7.2 IMPOSTER SYNDROME

> *"Woman up! Have confidence in yourself.*
> *So many women don't"*

Imagine two peers, equivalent in experience, expertise and competence. Professionally identical in every way, other than their genders. And - crucially - how they are perceived by their colleagues. For their colleagues assume that the man knows what he's doing until he messes up and is found out, and that the woman does not until she proves her worth. The assumption is that the man is **innocent until proven guilty**, whilst the woman is **guilty until she proves herself to be innocent**. In a court of law this disparity would be outrageous and unthinkable. Why then is it accepted and commonplace in the workplace?

Perhaps not surprising then that, according to a 2023 survey of 5,000 individuals conducted by Executive Development Network, women are more likely than men to experience imposter syndrome, with 54% of women affected and 38% of men.

> *"I have constant imposter syndrome.*
> *I think I'm winging it all the time"*

Imposter Syndrome is very common, surprisingly so amongst high achievers who live in fear of being found out, believing their success is down to luck rather than skill. In her book *'The Secret Thoughts of Successful Women: Why Capable People Suffer From the Imposter Syndrome and How to Thrive in Spite of It'*, Dr Valerie Young investigates this phenomenon and categorises imposter syndrome into five subgroups:

- the **Perfectionist** experiences major self-doubt when they fail to reach their excessively high goals

- the **Superwoman** pushes herself extra hard to make up for her shortcomings

- the **Natural Genius** believes if it doesn't come naturally, you are not worthy

- the **Soloist** refuses assistance in order to prove her own worth

- the **Expert** fears being exposed as inexperienced or unknowledgeable

suggesting different techniques to combat each particular flavour. And her choice of title is particularly apposite, given that, in the workplace, women are guilty until proven innocent.

> *"To tackle imposter syndrome, seek out a good boss. Someone who enables you to shine. If you don't shine, you lose confidence and you become less able to do your job. A vicious circle"*

> *"Some men don't know how to give feedback to women. I have learnt to live without honest feedback. You have to develop that awareness, that self-reliance and self-belief. You have to work it out"*

Female imposter syndrome is amplified by another psychological phenomenon, in which men overestimate their expertise whilst women understate theirs.

7.3 CONFIDENCE V EXPERTISE

> *"We have to be better than men. We have to prove ourselves"*

"Let me interrupt your expertise with my confidence."

Figure 7.1 - Confidence v Expertise
Copyright: © CartoonStock.com

> *"That's very good thinking you know. Turn on the Improbability Drive for a second without first activating the proofing screens. Hey, kid, you just saved our lives, you know that?"*
>
> *"Oh," said Arthur, "well, it was nothing really .."*
>
> *"Was it?" said Zaphod. "Oh well, forget it then. OK, computer, take us in to land."*
>
> **- from *The Hitchhiker's Guide to the Galaxy*, by Douglas Adams**

There is a well-documented phenomenon in the field of psychological research[27], which persists across multiple samples, ages, ethnicities and cultures: when asked to estimate their own intelligence, males frequently provide higher estimates than females. This has been termed the Male Hubris, Female Humility Problem[28] and it is all the more fascinating because males and females do not differ in general intelligence levels (although there are some gender disparities in specific cognitive abilities[29], such as verbal and visual-spatial tasks, and at the tails of the bell curve of intelligence distribution, where there are more men than women at both extremes).

There are many social conditioning phenomena which reinforce this belief, despite girls consistently outperforming boys academically at school. A fascinating example of this embedded bias is Seth Stephens-Davidowitz's 2014 research for the New York Times into commonly searched phrases. This revealed that parents are two-and-a-half times more likely to type into Google *"Is my son gifted?"* than *"Is my daughter gifted?"* Similar biases existed for other words relating to intelligence, such as 'genius'.

27 Reilly D, Neumann DL, Andrews G. Gender Differences in Self-Estimated Intelligence: Exploring the Male Hubris, Female Humility Problem, Frontiers in Psychology, February 2022
28 Furnham A., Hosoe T., Tang T. (2001). Male hubris and female humility? A cross-cultural study of ratings of self, parental, and sibling multiple intelligence in America, Britain, and Japan. Intelligence 30 101–115
29 Halpern D. F. (2011). Sex Differences in Cognitive Abilities, 4th Edn. Mahwah, NJ: Erlbaum

Small wonder then that by the time we are adults in the workplace, we have a deep-seated belief that men deserve their seat at the table, whilst women are lucky to have theirs.

> *"I'm nervous about changing jobs. I overplay the*
> *things I can't do, rather than blagging my way in"*

DUNNING-KRUGER EFFECT

These gender-based insecurities are further reinforced by the Dunning-Kruger effect,[30] the phenomenon whereby a person's lack of knowledge and skill causes them to overestimate their own competence, as illustrated in this widely available graphic (Figure 7.2).

It is particularly concerning in a workplace context because, not only are overconfident individuals extremely resistant to being taught, but they are also guilty of sharing the most - often misguided - information.

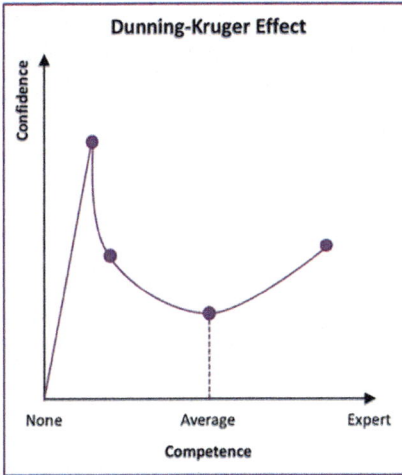

Figure 7.2 - Dunning-Kruger Effect
Source: Wikipedia

30 Kruger, J., & Dunning, D. (1999). Unskilled and unaware of it: How difficulties in recognizing one's own incompetence lead to inflated self-assessments. Journal of Personality and Social Psychology, 77(6), 1121-1134

Sadly, this can result in a vicious cycle for our already humble female worker, as believing she is less intellectually capable has a detrimental impact on her motivation levels, particularly in female-under-represented fields.[31] All of which is useful background in helping us to understand 'The Authority Gap'.[32]

7.4 THE AUTHORITY GAP

"That's an excellent suggestion, Miss Triggs.
Perhaps one of the men here would like to make it."

– Duncan Riana, Punch 1988

"Age is an issue first, and then gender.
The combination of the two is really hard"

It is a frustrating fact that women are not afforded the authority that their experience and expertise merit. Feeding imposter syndrome and festering a deep sense of injustice, this 'Authority Gap' manifests in many ways.

MANSPLAINING

Perhaps an inevitable consequence of the 'Male Hubris, Female Humility' effect, the act of a man patronising a woman with an explanation of a very basic concept, or one in which she is the expert, has become so commonplace and so derided that it has its own deliciously-coined verb.

---

31 (Dweck, 2002), (Kornilova, 2009), (Reilly and Hurem, in press)
32 'The Authority Gap: Why Women Are Still Taken Less Seriously Than Men, and What We Can Do About It' - Mary Ann Sieghart, Black Swan, 2022

> *"The mansplaining element is HUGE. With seniors, it is really valuable, but with peers and juniors it's like they think I've come out of nowhere with no experience. They tell me the most basic stuff. Can older males role model this?*

SPOKEN OVER

Similarly, women are not listened to, or spoken over, even when they are the acknowledged subject matter expert.

> *"Men talk over me in meetings and position themselves as 'the expert' in a way that they don't with other men"*

> *"Women are politer, so they let people speak over them. My wife has a PhD and she waits to speak even though it is her area of expertise, and still she gets talked over. Chairs need to do more to stop this from happening"*

> *"Women tend to be less forceful in discussions, are often more hesitant to express their opinions and have to fight to be heard. I find that the conversation is set at a rhythm that the men are happy with, and I am about to speak when a man jumps in"*

Case Study: School Quiz Night

I went to my son's school's quiz night - I'd been looking forward to it. There were four couples on our team, we'd never met before, and there was no discussion about who was good at what. Instead we slipped easily into gender stereotypes, with the men supplying the answers and the women dutifully writing them down. Apart from the round on chocolate, on which the women - obviously - led.

Then there was a question about 1977 Star Wars. There's nothing I don't know about that film - I must have watched it 200 times and I could recite the entire script off by heart. But they did not believe my answers, overrode me and wrote down something different which was, of course, incorrect. I realised that if I wanted to be believed, I had to explain *why* I came to possess that particular piece of general knowledge, like the reason that I knew 'Alperton' was the right answer was because I had spent every summer there when I was little. It wasn't until there was a maths question and my husband stepped in to say: '*Sorry, why aren't you listening to the Cambridge mathematician*?' that they started taking me seriously.

MISJUDGED

There is often an assumption that a woman is junior to her male colleague. Sometimes she is afforded so little status that she is excluded from the conversation entirely, not even afforded eye contact.

> *"People assume that the men I attend meetings with are more senior"*

> *"Being attractive and petite is a problem. A lot of men think they need to protect me. And then they realise I'm a fireball"*

> *"A new joiner directed his question to my junior, rather than to me. He wouldn't even look at me. I told the CEO who laughed it off, telling me that I was probably being intimidating. But I spoke to him about it. I don't accept bad behaviour. I call it out when I see it"*

STOLEN CREDIT

From contributing an idea in a meeting which is ignored until a male colleague repeats it - and is praised for it - moments later, to keeping your successes under wraps only to find a male colleague has stepped in and taken the credit, this everyday plagiarism happens in plain sight, is overlooked and thus implicitly is encouraged.

> *"I did all the work to get a fund buy-rated by an external consultant, on the back of which we got lots of investors. But the male salesperson got all the credit. I complained to my boss and he told me it was my fault, that I should have told everyone. I hadn't realised it was a pissing contest"*

7.5 DISSONANCE

"People don't like powerful women. They like a biddable, mid-career woman who bumps up their diversity statistics"

Case Study: The Female CEO

As a fairly forthright, 5'10 CEO with lots of authority, some elements of my style are more like a man than a woman and I was told it was making the men uncomfortable. I wasn't trying to be a man with tits; I was just being me, wanting to get on with my job!

There was so much confusing feedback - do it like this, do it like that. But you can't please everybody and I was unsure how to accommodate it all. I try not to be defensive, to listen, to be curious, to put it in the right bucket, asking myself: "*How much is this about me being a woman, and how much of it is about me being me?*"

I realised I needed to be more aware of the men's lived experiences if I wanted to be successful.

Somewhere deep within our psyche, there is something uncomfortable - dissonant - when a person of one gender displays traits of the other. Despite the progress made with LGBT+ rights in many cultures, more 'feminine' men are still at risk of attack. And telling a man he is behaving like a girl or a woman is a pretty damning insult.

Similarly, we don't like it when women display alpha male traits. This is particularly problematic in a work environment because the very behaviours that are emblematic of good leadership in a man just don't seem to sit right in a woman.

Our perceptions are gender-dependent. Where the man is assertive, the woman is aggressive. The man is determined, the woman is stubborn. The man is commanding, the woman is controlling. Ambition and competitiveness in a man are positives; they are highly undesirable - and unfeminine - in a woman. Broadly, if a woman's leadership style has masculine notes, she is condemned for it. Women are supposed to be nurturers. We just don't like the dissonance.

> *"Women are told to promote themselves, but then get criticised when they do. They need to be more elegant than men, balancing humility and self-promotion, being articulate and quietly confident"*

Case Study: Tall Poppy Syndrome

I had been at the firm for six months and was invited to co-present with the chair at a large global event for 600 directors. I was better than him. I hadn't meant to upstage him, but I didn't think to temper my performance. The audience loved it, but the board and chair hated it. They went on to mete out a series of small punishments and the next item I brought to the board was not approved. They literally cut me down to size. I was cautioned to be slow and safe, not to rock the boat. I felt naive that I hadn't tempered myself and played the politics. Behaviour that would be judged bold and courageous in a man is treated as slightly unhinged in a woman.

They then went on to leverage those very abilities during the pandemic, when I became the face of the firm on regular zoom calls to tens of thousands of staff. I did the emotional lift-and-shift to keep people going. I was utterly exhausted, whilst the rest of the board sat there during lockdown whilst their wives literally served them tea and scones.

Now I work with the FTSE 100 c-suite and the women constantly question themselves. I find I can't sit there with my hand on my heart and tell them it's all worth it.

Do women need to curb their more masculine traits to succeed?

> *"The best women I know have found their own authenticity and have been able to tap into it. Not the women who are masquerading as men"*

And to what extent should they curb their feminine tendencies?

> *"Whistle, don't cry. People might think you're mad, but that's better than them thinking you're emotional"*

> *"Don't be afraid to show vulnerability or femininity.
> Compassion is really important"*

My reference group's advice at times felt overwhelming, conflicting and sometimes measured. This in itself is an indication of how challenging we find the dissonance.

> *"You are a mature person and you have your innate
> management style. It's a bit like being a parent. You can tweak
> the way you parent, but you can't change it. It's instinctive"*

> *"If you can tap into your own authenticity,
> you will end up being happy"*

Perhaps recognising how uncomfortable we find dissonance, questioning why and challenging our reaction is the key.

Facing Up To It

8. CHANGING THE NARRATIVE

8.1 SUMMARY

1. The odds are stacked against women, but much of this is unintended and unrecognised bias. We can level the playing field by becoming aware of our biases and questioning their validity

2. Hybrid working supports working mothers and removes the stigma of juggling home and work life because it becomes invisible. Businesses that revert to a rigid, 'five days a week in the office' approach risk losing diversity in their workforce as working mothers vote with their feet

3. There is often prejudice against female bosses from both men and women

4. Queen Bee syndrome may exist, but it might just be that society views competition between women more harshly than between men. And perceived Queen Bee behaviours may come from a desire to bestow the learnings of years of hard-fought experience that doesn't land well

5. Women's high levels of nurturing and empathy can make them fantastic bosses

6. Women benefit enormously from role models, mentors and networks. Senior leaders should play their part, with men in particular proactively mentoring women

7. Men are becoming increasingly alienated by the drive for greater gender parity, with 47% thinking it has gone too far. To combat this, it is helpful to stress that diversity benefits men too, from an enhanced bottom line and from broader societal benefits

8. Male allyship is fundamental in achieving workplace equality. In practice, this can be as simple as calling out sexist behaviour, mentoring female colleagues, listening more and speaking less, and giving credit when its due

9. Quotas are one way of achieving diversity, but they can increase imposter syndrome and feel lazy and forced, and they can smack of tokenism. Changing the culture so we value diversity for its own sake is a healthier way of achieving gender equality

8.2 RECOGNISING BIAS

Thus far, through the lens of my reference group, it would appear that women draw the short straw...

Judged on their appearance, women experience sexual harassment, much of it low grade but some of it disturbingly not. They navigate through hormonal stormy seas which do not suit the 9-'til-5, Monday-to-Friday of office life. If they choose to have children, it is *their* bodies that go through the mill and it is *they* who end up doing the childcare heavy-lifting, in the background, unnoticed. For if it is noticed, they are penalised for it: for not being focused, for being less committed, even though it is precisely because of *their* gender's labours that male colleagues are able to get to their desks half an hour sooner, leave half an hour later and, worse still, raise an eyebrow as the women arrive 'late' and shirk off 'early', lured by the siren call of domestic chores. So, women have to be better, work harder, than their male equivalents just to earn a seat at the table. And even then they are spoken over, not listened to, not paid fairly. Then, just as they are beginning to make up for time lost on the career ladder through having children, menopause comes up and smacks them in the face. And on top of all that, they get hit by a higher incidence of pre-retirement cancer.

So. A question for you:

If you had the chance to go back to the moment of your conception and change sex, would you?

Fortunately, everything is nuanced; every yin has its yang, every weakness can also be a strength. So many of the stories that my reportage highlights arise not from malice or ill-intent, but from ignorance or unconscious bias. And by raising awareness, by pointing out the inequities, through male-driven peer pressure deeming them unacceptable, these will melt away.

Let's begin our quest to change the narrative. Let's recognise the biases.

> *"There's a ton of talk about glass ceilings in getting senior roles, equality or pay. But some of the time, it's the narrative you tell yourself. It can become self-fulfilling. Some of it is down to having children. But the rest is down to leaning out. I have made a conscious decision to do the opposite of what was expected. There is a silent societal expectation and I won't have it!"*

1. WOMEN ARE DIFFERENT

Men and women *are* different, but we are far more alike than not. If we examine where this prejudice first comes from, we can start to question why we are suspicious of the opposite sex. Perhaps it stems from our parents: how we saw them behave, or whether we had greater affinity for one than the other. Maybe it comes from a single sex upbringing, which led us to view the other sex as rarified creatures, fascinatingly and incomprehensibly otherly.

> *"I went to Southampton University in the late 1980s. My housemate and I were very different: he came from an all-boys' private school and was studying aeronautical engineering, whilst I'd been at a mixed comprehensive and was studying geography. I was very comfortable being in a mixed environment, but being around women was a big thing for him. I never had hang ups, always regarded woman as equal, never thought of them as 'only girls'"*

2. STAY-AT-HOME WIVES

A woman's place is in the home. Absolutely, if she wants it to be! But not if she doesn't. It should be her choice and those who don't believe this to be true should examine their 'why?'. Maybe they do genuinely believe that women are not entitled to a free choice or that they are somehow less capable at work and more capable in the home. Where does that belief come from? Or perhaps they feel threatened? Or was this the role modelling they witnessed as a child?

> *"Most of the men's wives didn't work, or had a hobby job: 'She earns pocket money to buy herself nice clothes'"*

> *"Men don't get it when they have a stay-at-home wife. For me, going to London on a business trip includes organising three days of home logistics. A lot of the men have a wife who packs their overnight bag for them. They don't have to give a second thought to whether their kids have tennis or a school project on the go"*

3. MEN LIKE THE STATUS QUO

The arguments against change are powerful. Short term, men benefit from the status quo, although it is unfair and unjust and not great for society or for businesses. And on top of that, change requires us to resist the comfortable armchair of inertia: it's just so much easier to do nothing or to put off doing something, rather than to take a stand now. But bad things happen when good people do nothing. Unless men proactively initiate change and embrace allyship, the world will stay the same.

> "Having kids has been a huge disadvantage to my career - it has massively impacted my ability to advance. There are assumptions made when you are a mother - that I couldn't do things at work because I'd have to do everything at home. I've had to over-compensate"

> "In every company, large or small, the tone comes from the top. Women will leave to find a culture where they can be themselves. We can only change if senior management wants it to change. We need more male allies saying this is really important"

> "Some men aren't going to change - they hate women at work. But that's about them, it's not about me"

4. WOMEN JUST AREN'T UP TO IT

> "I went to a women-only event at The Four Seasons. The panel included a woman who did a CEO job share and had to work late into the evening to make it seamless. There was one man on the panel. He was asked why there were no women on his board. And he replied - in front of an all-female audience, in front of this incredibly conscientious and successful CEO - that it was because there were no women good enough"

Maybe women *are* too soft for senior roles, perhaps because they care so much more - too much - about people's feelings. Maybe women *aren't* strong enough, dedicated enough, resilient enough. Maybe they *will* cry and leave early to go home to their kids.

It may be that women care more than men about other people's feelings. But why is it threatening? Maybe it's a good thing to have some emotional decision-making to counterbalance the logical. Perhaps we'd have fewer wars. And what does it matter if a woman does cry - that shows she is passionate and that she cares. Or if she leaves early - she will still get the job done. Maybe in a less linear manner, but what's so great about linearity? And as for not being strong enough or resilient enough - who has the babies? Who has to swim against the current all the time in a world designed by men, for men? Again, we must question our assumptions and where they come from.

5. MACHISMO

'*I threw an all-nighter last night.*' In some spheres, doing inhumanly long hours is still worn as a badge of honour, a status symbol. Working extreme hours has become a proxy for indispensability, commitment, success, or perhaps is a twisted measure of strength, virility and power.

Where on earth does this bias come from? Maybe the extreme workers are just inefficient and disorganised, with no place else to go. And does anyone genuinely believe they are immortal and immune, that their brains can function for prolonged periods with little or no sleep? This crazy idea needs to be challenged, particularly as stress and depression become ever-greater health risks. Without our health, we have nothing. And we certainly won't be able to deliver at work when we collapse with exhaustion.

6. IT'S ALL ABOUT THE BOTTOM LINE

It may well be, but focus on the bottom line could well be alienating the very people you need to deliver the bottom line you want. A better way to get results may well be via the indirect path of improving your culture and getting the balance right, challenging the dominant assumptions of presenteeism and machismo. If you have happy people who feel like they belong and are looked after, they are motivated to go the extra mile because they are genuinely engaged. And that needs diversity and the nurturing care that so many women bring to an organisation.

> *"Everything is related to billable hours. They are visible and an obsession. When times are tough, we don't get rid of the expensive billers, we get rid of the cheaper business services people, the reception staff"*

7. ITS ABOUT THEM, ITS NOT ABOUT YOU

Maybe the offensive comment *is* an egregious microaggression. But maybe it's not. Maybe we're being too sensitive. Maybe by telling ourselves a different, more helpful, back story, the problem goes away.

> *"We had an all-male dealing desk. It wasn't that they were ignoring me, it was just that they were talking about football all the time. So I leant in and learned about it. It's good courtesy - empathy - I built a good rapport"*

8. THE TRODDEN PATH IS THE ONLY PATH

The trodden path may be the safest path, the one with least risk attached to it because we know where it leads. But if it leads to nowhere, is it still the right one to take? Maybe it would be less risky to take a risk, to plough our own furrow, to see where it leads.

> *"I hit 30, had two kids and lost 10 years of career advancement. If I hadn't had them, I'd be a Chief People Officer of a large agency by now. But I carved a niche for myself instead. Sure, I would have been more high profile and influential, but I wouldn't be any more senior or richer. Having kids has played a big part in what I've achieved"*

> *"I'm not a signing partner. It was too intensive, too difficult for me to meet the impossibly-short client delivery deadlines alongside my family commitments. So instead I lobbied for the creation of a technical partner role, which is not client-facing but instead has other management responsibilities. And there is no difference in perception now"*

> *"I've taken barriers more as opportunities than challenges. I swerved around them. You don't have to follow the conventional path! You can define your own, one that works for you"*

8.3 HYBRID WORKING

> *"My husband has worked from home since our kids were 2 and 4 - they're now 18 and 20. So we did a complete role reversal and as a result we haven't faced the same challenges of work/life juggling that so many face. Over half of the senior women in my organisation have got a similar set-up"*

Before 2020, flexibility in the workplace was a rare thing indeed. You might work from home on the very odd occasion to handle a domestic emergency, but it was frowned upon and the assumption was that you'd have your feet up in the garden. COVID changed all that, showing us it was perfectly possible to work productively from home. And this was fantastic news for those juggling work and caring responsibilities.

> *"Flexible working made a huge difference. It was no longer visible when you needed to do home stuff, no more narrative of the stereotypical woman leaving early to rush off to do parents' evening"*

Now the working world is finding its new norm, and many businesses have settled on a 3-days-in/2-days-out pattern, with flexibility. Whilst this solves one problem for the juggling woman, it introduces another - proximity bias.

PROXIMITY BIAS

> **Case Study: Lunch with the CEO**
>
> The office working pattern had settled at four days in the office, with most people working from home on a Friday. A graduate in his mid 20s was coming in five days a week, even though he was the only member of his team to do so. When asked why, he explained that he got to have lunch one-on-one with the CEO every week.

A canny young man who will, no doubt, go far. And whilst we should applaud his resourcefulness in exploiting an opportunity that others have overlooked, to what extent should we be concerned that the same opportunity may not be available to those with childcare responsibilities on that Friday who are still, predominantly, women?

This raises the broader issue of proximity bias, whereby managers form tighter bonds and are more aware of the skills of those whom they spend regular time with. Good managers will be aware of, and adjust for, their inherent biases, and this is a new one for them to have on their radar. They can then proactively adjust their behaviours to spend more time with those who come in less frequently.

Some workplaces, however, have pulled it right back and are demanding five days in the office.

> *"Pre COVID, I was very flexible about people working from home. Then one of my team sent a photo of her wedding dress fitting on her working from home day. What should I do? As a manager, you need to trust that people are working when they are supposed to be, it sets the tone for the team. So I called her out on it. If you can set the tone right, you can offer the flexibility. It's all about whether you trust the people you work with"*

> *"The suspicion is that if you're not in the office, you're not working. Women are hurt by the pullback from flexible working"*

1950s LIVING

In June 2023, Fortune ran an article with the headline

Ultra-wealthy heterosexual couples are living like the 1950s never ended

By ultra-wealthy, they meant the top 1% of households.

Based on 30 years of data,[33] academic research[34] revealed that men are the sole breadwinners in over half (53%) of such heterosexual couples, which is twice the rate of less affluent heterosexual couples. These super-rich men will have political power, and many of them will be very influential in the businesses from which their wealth was generated. They are the ones who will be driving hybrid working policies and the work/life balance agenda. Will they truly comprehend how much the hybrid working world's flexibility has benefitted working couples? Particularly if we factor in earlier research[35] showing that men with stay-at-home wives are less supportive of women in their own workplaces?

---

33 1989 to 2019 data from the Federal Reserve's Survey of Consumer Finances

34 Separate Spheres: The Gender Division of Labor in the Financial Elite by Jill E Yavorsky, Lisa A Keister, Yue Qian, Sarah Thébaud - Social Forces, Volume 102, Issue 2, December 2023, Pages 609–632

35 The Implications of Marriage Structure for Men's Workplace Attitudes, Beliefs, and Behaviors toward Women by Sreedhari D. Desai, Dolly Chugh, Arthur P. Brief - Sage Journals, Volume 59, Issue 2

> *"During COVID we moved to an office that is difficult to get to without a car. It's a 10-minute walk through an industrial estate from one station, or a 40-minute walk through a wooded area to the other. It's not right to expect people, particularly women, to come into the office if their safety is compromised, particularly in the winter months"*

Lockdown was terrible for so many reasons.[36] But it did teach us that we could work effectively from home and that, indeed, some tasks are better-suited to be done in the quiet and sanctity of your own private space. So I ask you to use your power and influence to encourage the organisations you are associated with to help those who need it to retain flexibility in their lives and enable diversity in the workplace.

> *"People are able to leave the office earlier than they did, as they are set up to work from home"*

8.4 FEMALE BOSSES

> *"In my experience, women-on-women relationships either work really well or go horrifically wrong"*

> *"On my first day in a new job, my PA told me that she had only had one female boss before and she had sworn she would never have another. I said that sounded like it had been a terrible experience and asked what had happened. 'She used to go out and get drunk every lunchtime'. To which I replied, 'Yes, that must have been very challenging. Out of interest, why did you decide you never wanted another female boss, rather than another alcoholic boss?'"*

---

36 'On Motivation: Purpose & Hybrid Working', Jenny Segal, kdp 2023

141

> *"I [female] will never again work for a female boss. In my experience, they have treated it as a competitive relationship. But I love managing women, mentoring women"*

Women can be hugely supportive of each other, forming strong loyalties, allegiances and networks. They can also be deeply suspicious of each other, particularly where they are in the minority.

> *"The leadership shadow is something you can't easily control. If you're in charge of a team of six, the perception of you and your intent are well-aligned. But as you get more senior, the two diverge"*

Case Study: The Bullying Female Boss

I had a new boss, a woman with a child of a similar age to mine. It was a difficult relationship. She would play mind games with me, at first telling me to do something, then telling me not to do it. I started writing myself emails so I had a date-stamped audit. She was very good at managing upwards and the men loved her. But she was awful to me, and to other women, regularly making us cry. I would have left the firm, but I couldn't because I was pregnant. Several years after we stopped working together, she approached me at an industry event and I was so shaken just at the sight of her that I started sweating profusely.

It feels harder to resolve women-on-women conflicts. My hope is that there can be more support for women from women. It's about sharing, being honest about the challenges, being mindful of Queen Bee tendencies. Don't let us in-fight. We need to champion each other.

Queen Bee Syndrome:

"a term used to describe a workplace phenomenon in which a high-ranking female employee, usually a manager, intimidates and excludes her female subordinates, often leading to a hostile and uncomfortable work environment"

– Pelago

"I was in my late 20s, being interviewed for a job. I'd got through five intense rounds to meet with a senior female in her early 50s, a queen bee type. She said: 'Can I just ask what a child is doing in front of me?' I said: 'I've just got through five rounds of interviews! I've earned a seat at the table!'"

Honey, Honey

Copyright © 2024 Jenny Segal

Who springs to mind when you think about Queen Bees?

Margaret Thatcher (Figure 8.1) is perhaps the obvious candidate. She certainly fits the classic stereotype of the intimidating older woman, a female pioneer in the male-dominated world of 1970s and 1980s British politics who famously blocked the progress of other women, running an all-male Cabinet[37] for much of her time in office.

Figure 8.1 - Margaret Thatcher
Source: pixabay

However, context is king: when Thatcher became prime minister in 1979, there were only 19 female members of Parliament, of whom just eight were Conservatives with almost none of them sufficiently senior to hold Government office.

> *"Some females have had to overcome so much that they've over-corrected and become like men"*

Theories abound about whether Queen Bee Syndrome exists in {senior women-on-junior women} relationships to any greater extent than in the {senior men-on-junior men} dynamic. There is certainly no disparaging name for this type of behaviour in males, so it may just be that society judges women more harshly for displaying a competitive streak. We can easily construct a plausible narrative of a Queen Bee personality, shaped by hard-won fights to achieve career success and personal sacrifices around family choices. Instead of being pleased for the upcoming generations of women whose path they forged, our Queen Bee has become bitter, Miss Havisham[38]-esque, begrudging others the easy opportunities that she herself was denied.

---

37 the senior decision-making body of the UK Government
38 the wealthy spinster in Charles Dickens' 'Great Expectations', determined to revenge her heartbreak on the next generation

Throw in the misogynistic angle of jealousy and Queen Bee Syndrome becomes even spicier: the fading star reluctant to admit that her time is done and to step aside to make way for the new talent. Have a look at the jaw-dropping '*Happy Days Are Here Again / Get Happy*' duet[39] on The Judy Garland Show and you might catch a whiff of Garland's melancholy at Barbra Streisand's rising star and the fear of her own impending obsolescence.

So perhaps some of our Queen Bee's hardness is perception rather than fact. Perhaps it comes from a good place. Harsh, unwelcome advice, maybe about how to dress appropriately, might indeed stem from jealousy of a potential rival. But, alternatively, it could come from a place of mentorship, the desire to bestow unwelcome advice gleaned from years of hard-won experience and world-weary wisdom. Back to Garland and Streisand: despite their 20 year age gap, the two purportedly became friends after their recording and, in her memoir 'My Name is Barbra',[40] Streisand recalls:

> "I remember her saying something I never quite understood: '*Don't let them do to you what they did to me.*' I should have asked her what she meant, but I didn't want to appear too nosy"
>
> **– Barbra Streisand**

Garland died tragically of an overdose just six years later, aged 47.

> "*I think about Sheryl Sandberg's 'Lean In': this is not the way it should be, but it's the way it has to be until it's the way it should be. You might need to behave in a way that you don't want to. But try to do so in a way that doesn't damage future generations*"

---

39 From 'The Judy Garland Show' taped 4th October 1963
40 My Name is Barbra, Barbra Streisand, Century 2023

> *"You're going to be a role model, whether you like it or not. So think about what sort of a role model you want to be"*

Many of the 67 women in my reference group highlighted their emotional intelligence as the key female trait that enhances their performance at work, especially when they are in management roles. Their ability to nurture and empathise can make them exceptional managers, provided that the workplace culture recognises the value of management and encourages these traits to thrive.

> *"When I was a new graduate, I went out to a bar with a male colleague and picked up the wrong coat on the way home. The next day, we were all laughing about it. Then a female mentor took me out for lunch and pointed out the narrative that was developing about me - that I had a reputation as a party girl, was becoming the butt of jokes and was not being taken seriously. I was really grateful for her advice and took it on board"*

> *"I haven't experienced queen bee syndrome. Quite the opposite. I have been positively singled out by a senior woman who saw something in me that I didn't recognise in myself, and it leapfrogged me in my career. During my undergraduate internship, the (female) Head of Fixed Income sponsored me to apply for a graduate job. I wouldn't have done it otherwise. I hadn't been to private school. I didn't come from that world. And a few years later, I volunteered to be part of a network and she asked me to chair it. It gave me exposure to the CEO and really built my confidence"*

Case Study: Brutal Honesty

I've learnt that people like working for me. But maybe not in the moment, as my number one rule of management is to be brutally honest with my feedback. We kill people with kindness, thinking we are protecting them by not telling them how they are perceived. I'll go in with a view, listen carefully and give my opinion. I grow too.

Once I was talking to a younger male colleague about how he was dressing for work and he replied: *"Are you really telling me I have to dress like an old white man to get on in this firm?"* And I realised that I was dressing the way I did because I was trying to hide in the room. Now I wear red shoes with a black dress to counteract that.

It can be difficult when you're managing up. There are only two or three mountains you can die on each year, so you have to pick which ones you tackle. Sometimes I've had to tell my team: *"This isn't the best decision we've made as a firm, but it's not one I'm prepared to die for, so let's rally."*

Another time, I found out a colleague had been approving their own holiday and it made me question how trustworthy they were. When I challenged them, they told me: *"But you're always so busy."* And it was true. By being honest you get to the heart of the issue; you learn there's often more to it and you can have a real conversation.

Being a superb manager is akin to being a nurturing parent. Knowing when to handhold, and when to step back. Being encouraging and supportive, whilst engineering opportunities for growth. Being able to deliver both flavours of feedback - praise and critique - with a statesman's-like diplomacy that allows it to be received with dignity, acceptance, self-reflection and learning. This is incredibly difficult and requires incredible skill. And it is a skillset in which women, with their heightened levels of empathy,[41] have a natural advantage over men.

---

41   Meshkat, M., & Nejati, R. (2017) - Does Emotional Intelligence Depend on Gender? A Study on Undergraduate English Majors of Three Iranian Universities. Sage Open, 7(3)

8.5 FINDING YOUR TRIBE

> *"Women are amazing at having each other's backs. Bonding over an issue, you find your tribe. You get explicit support"*

Case Study: Strangers on a Train

It was early evening, rush hour on the tube. The carriage was really crowded. A group of passengers fought their way onto the train, edging up the aisle. A very tall, muscly man in his late 30s turned aggressively towards a middle-aged woman and demanded that she apologise for pushing him. She maintained that she hadn't - it was the normal commuter hustle. He became more aggressive and said to her: *"You need to apologise to me, I'm a man!"* That was it. A very slight young woman standing next to her was outraged and pulled him up on it. He squared up to her and it was pretty intimidating given the difference in their frame size, but she stood her ground.

And then another woman joined in, proclaiming that she was a lawyer so he had better watch out. For a moment he seemed to be weighing up his options and then he backed down, getting off the train at the next stop. The women were elated, and the strong bond of allyship they had formed in standing up to a sexist aggressor was apparent.

ROLE MODELS

When I was applying for my very first graduate job, the market was buoyant and I had a choice of offers. Without a second thought, I plumped for the (only) firm that had female partners. Long before the phrase was coined, I was exemplifying the *'You can't be what you can't see'* mantra, famously popularised by American civil rights activist Marian Wright Edelman in her 2011 Sundance documentary, 'Miss Representation'. Edelman is an impressive mould-breaker; in 1964, she became the first African-American woman to be admitted to the Mississippi bar and in 1971 she was the first black woman to be appointed to Yale's board of trustees.

It takes someone of Edelman's extraordinary vision, fortitude and drive to be what they can't see. We are not all as brave. And that's precisely why we need role models.

> *"I looked at the senior women in my firm, all childless, and actively thought: 'You clearly can't do this job with kids'. Over time, the company changed and that has changed my perception. We now have a female CEO, deputy CEO, and Chief People Officer, all great role models and examples of how work-life balance has been achieved"*

MENTORS

When we get stuck, we often need mentors to help us find our way, bestowing impartial advice willingly and selflessly that can allow us to navigate unfamiliar and difficult situations.

The best mentorship relationships develop organically, where there is a natural connection between mentor and mentee, perhaps because the mentee reminds us of our younger self. But really helpful mentorships can be engineered, through organised programmes and by potential mentors actively deciding to seek out a mentee. Male mentor/female mentee relationships can be particularly valuable in overcoming work-placed gender biases.

> *"Women worry about how they're perceived. Men aren't even having these thoughts. We need to mentor women to give then confidence, to look at what they are doing in a different way, to be compassionate to themselves and help them overcome their 'gold star syndrome', that societal aspect driving us to want to be the good girl"*

> "When you find your tribe, your cohort, you can flourish and grow. I worked with a senior woman who really helped me, much more than a male would. When I lost my mum, she could really relate and she opened up about her personal life. She mentored me generously. Before my first partner meeting, she warned me that they'd think I wouldn't have enough experience and she armed with what to say in response. But she never showed me favouritism in dishing out roles. I've taken this on in my management style"

> "I had an 'accidental' male mentor and ambassador, who spotted I had a flair for business development when I was manning a stand at a conference. He made an enormous difference, helped to remove obstacles, gave me profile and responsibility and hugely boosted my confidence. I had massive imposter syndrome, but he helped to get me recognised and that was my pathway to partnership"

NETWORKS

There can a particular joy in a certain type of all-female gathering, typified by camaraderie, an awareness of shared experience and a desire to share and learn. To help each other out without agenda, without expectation of a favour returned. Women seem to be particularly open to creating this kind of environment and so there are plenty of industry networks that allow them to connect and thrive. We just have to look.

> "My advice to younger women: have the confidence to be yourself. Work hard and let the work speak for itself. Develop mentors, allies. Put yourself forward even when you think you're not 100% qualified. And network! Build your cohort"

> "At 50, women's careers kick off. Your kids are off at university. You know your own space. The next ten years are the big ones. As we become more established, we network with other supportive woman and finally there are enough of us to play the woman card with. It's our equivalent of the golf club, going to the pub, 'How's the wife?'"

> "Discovering women's networks has been a joy. The camaraderie of women in a very male sector, solidarity with really smart women. Far from moaning, it's about being progressive, not retrospective, how can we make it better"

> "I have made really good friendships with women in the industry. They are peers, friends, that I can bounce ideas off. Women are open to this, sharing, helping each other"

8.6 ALL ABOUT MEN

> "I've never felt threatened by women, I've never been discriminatory. But have I reflected enough on the differences?"

AVOIDING ALIENATION

> "I was sitting on the train when a woman with a broken leg asked me for my seat. She had walked past several women to approach me, even though I was the oldest person in the carriage. I pointed this out and she was shocked at herself, saying: 'Oh my God - I thought I was a feminist'"

Men are being alienated by the drive to further gender equality, with a 2024 IPSOS survey[42] showing that 47% of British men think the cause of gender equality has gone too far, Gen Z[43] being particularly polarised at 60%.

---

42   IPSOS survey published in 2024
43   those born between 1997 and 2012

> *"At DE&I events, there is consistently low turnout from men - you're lucky if you get 20%. This only changes if you frame the event in a way which suggests it is not about women"*

Men worry about the economic impact on them of gender parity. Senior men fear for their job prospects at a life stage when their age plays against them as well as their gender, and that it is becoming harder to be appointed into board roles. Younger men are alienated too, worrying about getting the same access to jobs and aware that it is that much harder to get a decent salary and get onto the housing market. A number have been affected by Andrew Tate's[44] toxic view of the world.

And beyond that, some men are struggling to see what the problem is because microaggressions have become so embedded that they do not notice them. Women resent the unfairness: the way that men's bad behaviour is often tolerated if they perform well elsewhere in the business; the way that they have to take maternity leave, whereas few men opt to take equivalent paternity leave as they recognise it may damage their career.

How do we bring people together when men just see a zero-sum game, thinking that striving for greater gender parity is bad for them?

In 'The Authority Gap', Mary Ann Sieghart highlights research that men in more gender-equal societies report higher levels of happiness and satisfaction in work and home life, and that female-led countries fared better in the COVID pandemic. And BCG research[45] illustrated that gender diversity resulted in companies that were more creative, resilient and innovative. So at a corporate level, achieving gender parity helps to achieve business success, increasing employment opportunities for men and women alike.

Beyond that, it's the right thing to do.

---

44 A self-proclaimed misogynist and social media influencer
45 The Rewards of an Engaged Female Workforce - BCG Focus, October 2016; How Diverse Leadership Teams Boost Innovation - BCG article, January 2018

> *"Some men behaved neutrally towards me at work, some were hostile and some went out of their way to be helpful. I found I had classified the latter into two groups: the ones who wanted to sleep with me and the ones who had daughters"*

> *"Where does allyship come from? From having daughters. I used to think it was hypocritical, that male colleagues were only behaving like allies because they had daughters. But now I think: 'Does it matter where it comes from?'"*

Businesses are working towards eliminating the gender pay gap and appointing more women into senior roles; their progress is becoming more transparent with increasing commercial pressures to publicise salary and gender make-up. But an arguably more powerful force is that of the social norm: making it apparent that it is unacceptable to treat women as inferiors. And this is where male allyship is fundamental to success.

MALE ALLYSHIP

"A male ally is a man who advocates for and supports marginalised groups in their fight for equality and social justice. Male allies can be especially important in the fight for gender equality, as they can help to transform harmful gender stereotypes and relations."

– AI Overview

> *"Having male allies works really well when they call out bad behaviour when it happens. Something as simple as: 'I notice you said that to [female]. Please can you explain that to me?' makes the person think, particularly if it comes from a place of curiosity. But all too often there are no allies or advocates in the room when it matters, or they come back to you after the event with words of support, rather than acting in the moment"*

Case Study: Ostracising Offenders

In an open plan construction site office of around 40 people, including just a handful of women, one of the site workers started making disparaging comments about the way one of the younger women was dressed. Without exchanging a word, the group in the immediate vicinity acted collectively to ostracise him. They edged him out, making it clear from their body language and positioning that his views were unwelcome, inappropriate and not held by the rest of them.

Acting as an ally is more straightforward than some people think. Helpful actions that men can take to support gender equality include:

- **recognising their advantage** (be willing to step back so that other voices can be heard)

- **educating themselves** on key issues related to gender inequality. There are lots of really accessible books on the topic, including the two that I have made reference to: 'The Authority Gap' by Mary Ann Sieghart and 'Invisible Women' by Caroline Craido Perez

- **speaking up**, calling out sexist behaviour when they see it

- **supporting** female colleagues through mentorship, helping them to progress, creating an environment in which they feel included and heard

- **listening,** by speaking less and giving women the opportunity to share their thoughts

- **giving credit** where it is due, proactively structuring projects so that women can shine and talking about talented women.

And it is very effective:

> *"A senior colleague undermined me to a client, introducing everyone via their job title, but with me he just said: 'She does something with projects'. I called it out to my male line manager who told him to be more aware of his language. I noticed a big change - he was more respectful with me. Although he didn't apologise to my face"*

> *"There's a big difference between the men and women I've worked with: men are significantly more confident about their ability, are uncomfortable to admit to their shortcomings and will grab an opportunity that they're not ready for. I encourage the women to do stuff outside their comfort zones"*

> *"Women tend to withdraw from the conversation when they're not heard. So I split a discussion into smaller groups to encourage them to speak. It only takes one or two people to speak over others for it to become a problem"*

Case Study: Becoming a Male Ally

Many men want to do the right thing, but they don't know what to do. The starting point is for them to work on their 'why': why is allyship important to them? Then they should educate themselves to really understand their male privilege, by reading books on everyday sexism, attending women's networks, checking potentially contentious communications with female allies before sending them, asking women for constructive feedback.

80% of leaders are men and 60% of managers are men; these men can mentor women and hire women.

The easiest way to make a difference is to call out bad behaviour when you see it. Women really appreciate it.

"We were standing in the office and my male colleague's chair started going down and he made a comment about me going down on him. All the blokes laughed. My cheeks were burning. It wasn't the first time he'd done it - he had a track record of being inappropriate with his female colleagues. I went to HR and they told me that either I could confront him or they would handle it. So I hauled him into a room, the blood drained from his face and he apologised. He has been very careful and respectful since. But the other men had a duty to say something"

Case Study: Allyship In Action

Men are used to being led by senior men, immediately discounting you for your gender. Navigating the 'bro network' is tricky as they hear *about* you more than they hear *from* you. And this can be loud, as there is lots of male undercurrent gossip when it comes to the appointment of senior women.

Over a period of 18 months, one of my much older, male direct reports tried to undermine me. He would challenge me regularly in an unconstructive way, and we couldn't have a team call without him picking over the tiniest detail. The other men picked up on it and raised it with him outside the meeting, saying his comments were gendered, with five out of eight on the call writing a letter of complaint to HR.

When allyship happens in the right way, behind the scenes like this, it's very powerful. When they're doing it because it's the right thing to do, not to be nice to you.

"My male manager had young kids, they'd been through IVF and his wife had been really ill throughout her pregnancy. He told me to go home when I was tired. He was incredibly supportive"

"We need more allies. Particularly the traditional guys who say it's important, because the other traditional guys listen to them"

> **Case Study: Clout Counts**
>
> I ran a property company with a male business partner and we had a very capable, highly qualified female project manager. Her male peers had no appreciation of how much more qualified she was than them. Even the builder felt he could question her authority. It wasn't until my business partner stepped in and said - no - enough - wind your neck in, that he backed down. It took senior male allyship to solve the situation. Being alert to the bias, calling it out and having the clout to stop it.

8.7 CULTURE V ENFORCEMENT

There has been a lot of noise and activity around DE&I, but its real-world impact on working practices is still too low. Many businesses make a fanfare about celebrating International Women's Day, but how many actually do anything tangible about it, with the 2024 Sexism in the City[46] report recognising woefully inadequate progress in addressing the sexism inherent in the financial services industry.

One way to try to get it right is to force action through regulation, requiring reporting to demonstrate compliance. There is a move towards this in the UK around defining and identifying 'non-financial misconduct' to identify and prevent bad behaviour and to stop serial offenders being forced out of one role with an NDA[47] in their back pocket to prevent anyone revealing the real reason for their departure, so they can land their next big role and continue their pattern of offensive abuse at their next place.

But there is a big difference between doing it because the Financial Conduct Authority says we have to, and doing it authentically because we want to, because we know it's the right thing to do. And because we recognise it will result in better outcomes for our businesses.

Valuing diversity is the stepping stone.

---

46   House of Commons Treasury Committee report - 8th March 2024
47   Non-Disclosure Agreement

There is plenty of research to evidence that cognitive diversity improves decision-making and innovation, both of which filter through to the bottom line and produce better business results. And increasing the number of female decision-makers is a simple solution to achieving it. And simultaneously, we end up with a more balanced culture, which reduces sexism.

If we change narrative around DE&I so we do it because it's good for the bottom line as well as for society, a lot of the problems go away.

Case Study: Promoting the Mini-Not-Me

When I joined the firm, it was an all-male partnership with a very masculine style. That was an advantage for me because of the affinity bias. Hiring in our own image, our 'mini-me', validates us, it feeds our ego. But I have always really appreciated differences. You need differences in your leadership composition, as men behave differently when the environment is all male, and statistically men are more interested in power.

My male partners thought I should try and manage a woman out of the business, that she wasn't a good fit for us. But she was incredible at relationships and I saw a different side to her as we had grown up in the business together. So instead I said: *"I trust you, I will step back."* She's now a partner, is doing brilliantly and it's working really well.

"We should apply positive action, thinking about what different people need to thrive. And then just suck up the pain of enabling them. Don't talk about the cost of diversity, talk about an investment in diversity"

> *"We have started tailoring our partner track to incorporate those on maternity leave. We need to recognise that treating everybody the same is not the way to achieve equity. Sameness does not equate to fairness"*

> *"The very real focus on diversity has thrown up leadership opportunities for women. But women spend a lot of time on the softer stuff like whether people are looked after, and the administration side, rather than on business development. This is not valued in the same way as business development and plays out overall as a negative for women's progression"*

The next question is how we go about achieving diversity in a way that is constructive, and doesn't create adjunctive problems such as disenfranchising the incumbent majority, imposter syndrome and tokenism.

QUOTAS

Should we have diversity quotas, whereby a specified percentage of those in post must come from a given minority?

The main argument in favour is that we need to do something radical to break the *'You Can't Be What You Can't See'* cycle, to get minorities through the door and into positions. This then creates a virtuous circle because, as well as balancing up the diversity scales, they act as role models for the next generation who will see that they too can be successful in that field. Which encourages them to apply for jobs and, in a generation or two, the problem is solved.

The argument against is that we are prioritising diversity over talent and thus our shortlist is peopled with compromise candidates. Our choice is constrained to individuals who are the right ethnicity/gender/background/etc, but who maybe aren't as strong as the ones we could pick from the widest pool. And to achieve optimal business outcomes, we should prioritise selecting the best person for the job in absolute terms, not the best person from a pool that has been filtered for appropriate diversity.

> *"We should appoint the best person for the team. We have become so focused on achieving diversity that we risk the disenfranchisement of people who are very experienced"*

This then compounds imposter syndrome for the appointed candidate which, if they are from a diverse minority group, they probably suffer from more than their fair share. It hits them in two ways. Firstly, they doubt themselves, thinking: *"Was I only picked because I'm the diversity candidate?"* And it damages their credibility with their new colleagues, who may well be thinking: *"They were only picked because they're the diversity candidate"* and thus afford them less respect and set a higher bar for them to prove themselves.

> *"The sales threshold for promotion to MD was £4m. I'd been posting £10m, so I got promoted. I was in my late 30s and my male colleague, a peer in his late 50s, told me: 'You must have been the diversity statistic'"*

The theory of abundance is a useful counter to this. It proposes that there are enough resources to go around. True, we may need to cast the net wide enough to find them, but that is a question of the time and money we have available to make the appointment. An extreme example helps to illustrate the point. Suppose we decide we want to go so über-diverse that we want to appoint an off-world alien. Assuming our universe is infinite (roll with me on this one!), statistically there *will* be super-evolved lifeforms out there somewhere that would be the ideal fit. We may have to conquer time and space travel to find them, but we are on a mission, our budget and timescale are unbounded, so it's all good! The point is, with a wide enough net, we *will* find enough excellent candidates for a fantastic shortlist of talented, skilled AND diverse individuals.

> *I don't think we should have quotas. It's not sustainable, it's lazy.*

> **tokenism** *noun*:
>
> "the practice of making only a perfunctory or symbolic effort to do a particular thing, especially by recruiting a small number of people from under-represented groups in order to give the appearance of sexual or racial equality within a workforce"
>
> **– Oxford Reference**

Tokenism is the dark side of the quota, the evil twin of inclusion. On the face of it, you're being offered a great opportunity, but it's pretty obvious it's not authentic.

> *"I was once invited to join a committee, and was told it would be really helpful to have me on it as I was young and female. No mention was made of my ability. So I said no. I won't do tokenism"*

> *"I was working on a new business pitch and everyone was sensitive that the pitch team should not just consist of white men. I'd been a big contributor to the work, but the implication was that I was only there because I was a woman. The second time it happened, I called it out, pointing out that I bring more than my gender. There were huge amounts of remorse"*

> *"We host an annual conference over several days and the jewel in its crown is a dinner at a huge stately home in the country. We invite Chief Investment Officers from all over the world and your reputation as a salesperson rides on whether you can get your top contacts to attend, or there's a scar on your reputation. I had just joined the firm and was told that, even though I was an MD, I would not be attending as I didn't have any clients yet. On the final day of the conference, they called to ask if I could go along for the day because clients had complained there weren't any women present. I said no"*

The defining element of tokenism is that you are being selected simply because of your diversity value; even when you have the skills as well, they are not the reason for your selection. By accepting the token, are you grasping an opportunity to shine and change minds, or are you simply perpetuating the problem and embedding the prejudice?

If we get the culture right, if we value women as equals, the rest will start falling into place.

Scout

Copyright © 2024 Jenny Segal

164

9. IN CONCLUSION

The process of writing this book - devising and executing the interviews, researching the topic, constructing a narrative - has taken about six months. During that time, I have become immersed in the experiences of my reference group and increasingly alert to the casual gender injustices in our everyday world. And I have emerged more of a feminist than I expected, sensitised to the challenges women face every day, simply because of our biology and the way the world has morphed around it.

Some of that is for good reason. Over the 150 years from 1847, UK maternal mortality fell by 98%;[48] when couples swore 'til-death-us-do-part, it was a much more transitory promise. Perhaps then it is no surprise that women were lesser, objectified, a vessel to carry children into this world, more than likely to be broken by the process and the shards discarded.

But with the advent of contraception, with childbirth a much less deadly undertaking in the western world, women are able to control their biology, rather than it controlling them. We may have mastered our biological disadvantage, but we have yet to master its legacy.

Men, women need your allyship. And the world needs your allyship. Solving the environmental, political and economic issues our species is facing needs the diverse skills and thinking of both genders. This is your call to arms.

> *"I worry that we haven't made as much progress as we think. Yes, in the last five years we've hired loads of strong women. But we haven't dealt with innate biases. We haven't won that fight"*

---

48   Kerr RS, Weeks AD. Lessons from 150 years of UK maternal haemorrhage deaths. Acta Obstet Gynecol Scand 2015; 94: 664–668

LET'S TALK ABOUT SEX

1. Be actively on the alert for sexual harassment and be ready to step in to diffuse it by:

   - calling out inappropriate banter

   - joining a conversation if it is becoming intense

   - standing in the way of the harasser

2. Adopt an 'Ask for Angela'-type code phrase, enabling employees to flag their need for help

3. Introduce compulsory training and attestations as part of an annual 'Fit & Proper' checklist to eliminate sexual harassment at work

4. Make the sexual harassment reporting process painless and responsive. Ensure it sanctions offenders proportionately and sends a clear message that such behaviours are unacceptable

5. Issue suppliers with a written code of conduct specifying expected standards of behaviour

6. Shift from a *'Protect the business from being sued'* mindset to a *'Do the right thing for the employee'* mindset

THE MOTHERHOOD PENALTY

7. Men, ensure you are pulling your weight domestically. Equality for women in the workplace begins at home

8. Parents should take equal lengths of parental leave, regardless of their gender

9. Be sensitive to the challenges women face around fertility, including miscarriage and IVF which can be emotionally and physically devastating

10. Ease the transition back to work after parental leave by offering a well-structured 'Keeping in Touch' programme and by acting with sensitivity and kindness

11. Maintain maximum flexibility in working hours and location. Hybrid working helps working parents

'WOMEN'S PROBLEMS'

12. Provide sanitary products, disposable knickers and long black cardigans in female toilets

13. Raise awareness of miscarriage, so that colleagues can provide appropriate support

14. Offer menopause support through education, flexible working and sensitivity

15. Ensure private medical insurance includes menopause-related conditions

AGGRESSIONS - MICRO AND MACRO

16. Be alert to gender-biased infrastructure and provide alternatives, such as microphones that don't require pockets and name badges with lanyards

17. Use a common-sense approach to challenging microaggressions, using an

Intended/Not Intended

versus

Mild/Egregious

framework

18. Recognise and value the role of the 'office mum'

19. Vary networking events to offer a mix of before, during and after work timings, with a mix of cultural and sport options with broad appeal

20. Address the gender pay gap by eliminating it, not simply reducing it. The cost of losing and replacing disenfranchised females may well outweigh the cost of paying them fairly from the outset

21. Create opportunities for women to demonstrate what they can do, recognising that they are less likely to speak up or volunteer

GUILTY UNTIL PROVEN INNOCENT

22. Recognise your personal biases! We can level the playing field by becoming aware of our prejudices and questioning their validity

23. Ascribe authority based on expertise and experience, rather than gender. This will reduce mansplaining and taking credit for women's ideas

24. Recognise our dislike of dissonance, whereby traits we laud in men are unfairly lambasted in women

CHANGING THE NARRATIVE

25. Encourage networking, mentoring and role modelling for women. Senior men should proactively mentor their female colleagues

26. Male allyship is fundamental to achieving workplace equality. This can be as simple as calling out sexist behaviour, mentoring female colleagues, listening more and speaking less, giving credit when it is due and adopting and encouraging inclusive body language and eye contact

27. Quotas drive diversity, but they can increase imposter syndrome and smack of tokenism. Instead, change the culture so we value diversity for its own sake

Crock of Gold

*So many important ideas explored in a concise, practical and
genuinely engaging way. A great book for any would-be manager
and for all those who believe in building cultures which have
humans rather than 'resources' as their beating heart"*
Helen Franklin – Leadership Coach, Living Systems

*"A belter of a book. Good managers will enjoy its wisdom,
not least because it will help them to go from good
to great. Poor managers will benefit from immediate
improvement, if they are curious enough to read it"*
Paul Craven – Behavioural Science Specialist & Public Speaker

*"Jenny has a very engaging way of holding up a mirror for all of
us with responsibility for leading and motivating organizations
and teams, gently helping us identify opportunities to improve"*
Nate Dalton – Founder, Daybreak; Former CEO, AMG

*"This is a brilliant piece. Leadership writing can take too long
to hit the point, but this captures the components of great
and not-so-great leadership and the dynamics of fantastic
culture and team harmony in a terrific and easy read"*
Paul Price – CEO, MSIM Ireland

*"Intelligent and passionate, this brilliant book is thought-
provoking and immediately useful. Its style creates momentum,
making it an easily digestible read with important new ideas"*
Kate Philp – Director & Founder, Corran Consulting

"Essential reading if you want to run a successful team"
Hugh Cutler – Head of Business Development, Pollen Street

*"I love this book. The message is spot on: great workplaces
require great managers. Jenny provides the pathway"*
Jim Ware, CFA – Founder, Focus Consulting Group

"A thought-provoking capsule collection of the wisdom I wish I'd known 30 years ago. A must-read for new managers who care about culture, inclusion and excellence"
Sally Bridgeland – Chair, Impax Asset Management Group

"A must-read for any employee from entry-level to C-Suite, providing real-life examples that define and drive success"
Jeff Cerutti – Professor, Mercy College

"In a world where leadership and sustainability are so important, this is an essential read"
Debbie Clarke – Global Head of Investment Research, Mercer

"Accessible reading for leaders at all levels who genuinely wish to create a positive and thriving workplace culture"
Sharon Gregory – Director, Mental Health Services

ON MOTIVATION: PURPOSE & HYBRID WORKING

"The book of our time"
Imran Qureshi – Head of North America, WTW

"Jenny Segal's must-read sequel on motivation is packed with socially-researched insight, compassion and actionable ideas on how to make working life work wonderfully"
Calum Cooper – Chair of Partnership Council, Hymans Robertson

"Stimulates new ideas and concepts that we can all grasp and start working with straight away"
Michelle Elstein – Founder, Courageous Co.

"Very gripping, resonating with many experiences during lockdown. The poignancy of the stories about using your time wisely really struck home, inviting you to pause and think"
Paul Price – Founder & CEO, Haven Green

"This presents the divergence of views and preferences, helpfully illustrated by real life case studies and a nuanced discussion. The Work Wheel is a particularly helpful visual to ensure one's hybrid working experience is comprehensive and fulfilling"
Aoifinn Devitt – Chief Investment Officer, Moneta

"A thoughtful and thorough analysis of the implications of working remotely, along with observations from C-Suite executives on how this new paradigm affects culture and execution"
Jeff Cerutti – Professor, Mercy College

"Brilliantly engaging and insightful call to rethink how we work. Combining case studies, research and experience, this book offers a clear and practical toolkit to harness the best of old and new styles of working for happier and more productive workplaces"
Annabel Gillard – Organisational Culture & Ethics Expert

"Our firm works with financial organizations around the world, and all of them have asked for advice about hybrid work. Jenny's book provides the answers. Well written, fun to read, and powerfully informative. Highly recommended"
Jim Ware, CFA – Founder, Focus Consulting Group

ON MOTIVATION: BOARD EFFECTIVENESS & CULTURE

"Jenny's understanding of hybrid working brings board effectiveness up to date. Full of top tips"
Sally Bridgeland – Chair, Impax Asset Management

"A cracking book for boards which thrive on continual improvement. Full of tried-and-tested tips on how to build, evolve and get the best out of multi-disciplinary boards. I doubt there is a motivated board or chair out there that couldn't find something new to try in the spirit of making a positive difference"
Calum Cooper – Chair of Partnership Council, Hymans Robertson

"A comprehensive, fascinating, up-to-the minute guide to what is and isn't working in boardrooms, for seasoned and new NEDs alike"
David Semmens – CIO, Cadro & Non-Executive Director

"A distillation of very powerful and topical insights into governance and board effectiveness. A worthwhile read for any non-executive or executive for helpful tips and suggestions"
Paul McNamara – Non-Executive Director

"Illuminating insights into board dynamics, identifying best practice whilst challenging the status quo"
Annabel Gillard – Organisational Culture & Ethics Expert

"A thought-provoking and enjoyable read for anyone interested in improving their performance at board level"
Rosemary Beaver – Non-Executive Director

Through the Square Window

Copyright © 2024 Jenny Segal

175

BIBLIOGRAPHY

Adams, D. (1979). *The Hitchhiker's Guide to the Galaxy.* Pan Books.

Advance Pro Bono. (2021). *Prevalence and Reporting of Sexual Harassment in UK Public Spaces'.* APPG for UN Women.

Alderman, N. (2016). *The Power.* Penguin.

Brosnan, S. &. (2003). *Monkeys Reject Unequal Pay.* Nature.

Chung, W., Lim, S., Yoo, J., & Yoon, H. (2013). *Gender difference in brain activation to audio-visual sexual stimulation; do women and men experience the same level of arousal in response to the same video clip?* International Journal of Impotence Research 25, 138–142.

Clark, E. (2002). *The Human Face of Nicola Horlick.* BBC News.

Currey, M. (2013). *Daily Rituals: How Artists Work.* Knopf.

Furnham A, H. T. (2001). *Male hubris and female humility? A cross-cultural study of ratings of self, parental, and sibling multiple intelligence in America, Britain, and Japan.* Intelligence.

Halpern, D. (2011). *Sex Differences in Cognitive Abilities, 4th Edn. Mahwah, NJ: Erlbaum.* Psychology Press.

Krentz, M., Tracey, C., Tsusaka, M., Strack, R., Garcia-Alonso, J., Dosik, D., & Kilmann, J. (2016). *The Rewards of an Engaged Female Workforce.* BCG.

Kruger, J. &. (1999). *Unskilled and Unaware of It: How Difficulties in Recognizing One's Own Incompetence Lead to Inflated Self-Assessments.* Journal of Personality and Social Psychology.

Lorenzo, R., Voigt, N., Tsusaka, M., Krentz, M., & Abouzahr, K. (2018). *How Diverse Leadership Teams Boost Innovation.* BCG.

Meshkat, M. &.-D. (2017). *Does Emotional Intelligence Depend on Gender? Study on Undergraduate English Majors of Three Iranian Universities.* Sage.

Orwell, G. (1949). *1984.* Secker & Warburg.

Perez, C. C. (2019). *Invisible Women.* Vintage.

Reilly D, N. D. (2022). *Gender Differences in Self-Estimated Intelligence: Exploring the Male Hubris, Female Humility Problem.* Frontiers in Psychology.

RS Kerr, &. W. (2015). *Lessons From 150 Years of UK Maternal Haemorrhage Deaths.* Acta Obstet Gynecol Scand.

Segal, J. (2021). *On Motivation: Building Better Workplace Cultures.* kdp.

Segal, J. (2023). *On Motivation: Board Effectiveness & Culture.* kdp.

Segal, J. (2023). *On Motivation: Purpose & Hybrid Working.* kdp.

Sieghart, M. A. (2022). *The Authority Gap: Why Women Are Still Taken Less Seriously Than Men, and What We Can Do About It.* Black Swan.

Sreedhari, D., Chugh, D., & Brief, A. P. (2014). *The Implications of Marriage Structure for Men's Workplace Attitudes, Beliefs, and Behaviors toward Women.* Sage.

Streisand, B. (2023). *My Name is Barbra.* Century.

Yavorsky, J. E., Keister, L. A., Qian, Y., & Thébaud, S. (2023). *Separate Spheres: The Gender Division of Labor in the Financial Elite.* Social Forces.

Young, V. (2011). *The Secret Thoughts of Successful Women: Why Capable People Suffer From the Imposter Syndrome and How to Thrive in Spite of It.* Crown Currency.

Fly Trap

INDEX

Mother Earth II

Copyright © 2024 Jenny Segal

Printed in Great Britain
by Amazon